Arias & Raspberries

Sir Harry Secombe, CBE, was born in Swansea in 1921. After a spell as a pay clerk, he joined the Territorial Army and saw action in Sicily, Italy and North Africa, met Spike Milligan, and developed an interest in entertainment. Demobbed in 1946, he made his first professional stage appearance at the Windmill Theatre. Radio breaks followed, then came the celebrated *Goon Show* which was to acquire a cult following and turn Messrs Secombe, Milligan, Sellers and Bentine into household names. Secombe's ascent to the top of his profession continued through the variety theatre – five times topping the bill at the London Palladium; film roles including Bumble the Beadle in *Oliver!;* stage musicals – notably the title role of Pickwick in the West End and on Broadway; and numerous television shows, including the popular Sunday evening programme *Highway* and, more recently, *Songs of*

He has been married to Myra children and five grandchildren

For my family – I love them all

Also by Harry Secombe

Arias &
Raspberries

The Autobiography of
HARRY SECOMBE

Vol 1

'The Raspberry Years'

PAN BOOKS

First published in 1989 by Robson Books Ltd, London.

This edition published 1997 by Pan Books
an imprint of Macmillan Publishers Ltd
25 Eccleston Place, London SW1W 9NF
and Basingstoke

Associated companies throughout the world

ISBN 0 330 35463 9

3 5 7 9 8 6 4 2

A CIP catalogue record for this book is available from
the British Library.

Printed and bound in Great Britain by
Mackays of Chatham PLC, Chatham, Kent

CONTENTS

PREFACE

When a man delves into his past he glimpses a stranger who is vaguely familiar. Did I say that? Did I really do that? Only fragments of conversation come to mind and events become kaleidoscopic. One can only hope to reveal the essence of oneself, and embellishment here and there is inevitable.

An entertainer leaves little of himself behind after he has gone. A round of applause cannot be framed and a standing ovation cannot be displayed on a mantelpiece. The best memorial he can hope for is that at some time in the future a man in a bar may say to his companion, 'That Harry Whatsisname was a funny bloke, he always made me laugh.'

This book is for him.

CHAPTER ONE

Beginnings

Just as all true cockneys are born within the sound of Bow Bells, so all true Welshmen are presumed to have been born on a hillside.

My parents kept a welcome for me in Dan-y-graig Terrace, which lies along the slope of Kilvey Hill, Swansea. The date was 8 September 1921, and the time was midday. I was the third child, Frederick Thomas having arrived two years and eight months earlier, and my sister, Joan, about a year before I made my squalling entrance.

These facts are indisputable and can be verified, I'm afraid. I say 'I'm afraid', because for quite a while during my childhood I held the romantic notion that I was really a royal prince who had been left on the doorstep, and that one day the arrival at the door of a group of bemedalled important personages would signal the beginning of my reign.

I used to search my person for anything resembling a royal birthmark – a mole, or a wart, even, which would reveal to me my own true identity. The best I could come up with was a blind boil which I discovered on the back of my neck by arranging the mirrors on the dressing table.

When at the age of eight I turned yellow, I thought that my real colour had come through at last and that at any minute Oriental gentlemen in embroidered robes would come along to the council estate and bear me off on a litter to my rightful inheritance. Unfortunately, it turned out that I had jaundice.

After that, I became reconciled to the fact that I really was the son of a commercial traveller and that my mother was who she said she was.

At this distance my recollection of the time spent in Dan-y-graig Terrace is naturally pretty dim. I remember sitting on the back doorstep looking at the funnels of ships, and have a vague memory of wearing a long flannel nightgown and bouncing up and down on a bed with my brother. It is fairly reasonable that this period of my life should be difficult for me to reconstruct because we left the house – in which my parents only rented a couple of rooms from the Roberts family – when I was four years old.

We then went to live on a new council estate which was being built on the lower part of Kilvey Hill, about half a mile away. My memory of the day we moved into the new house is with me still. My mother was carrying my baby sister, Carol, in her arms, and my brother Fred and I ran alongside her. When we came to the top of St Leger Crescent, workmen were still busy on the other houses, and outside number 7 was a huge mound of rubble where the garden was supposed to be. My mother opened the freshly painted green gate and we all proceeded towards the equally freshly painted green front door with its new brass knocker. Mam opened it with her shiny new key and in we went. I remember looking with awe at all the space inside. There was a front room downstairs and beyond that a kitchen and a bathroom. A flight of stairs faced the front door and I climbed them timidly. At the top were three more rooms and a toilet. The immensity of the place intimidated me. I ran downstairs to my mother and asked her if I could go in all the rooms, because back in Dan-y-graig Terrace my brother and I were constantly being told not to open doors other than ours in the house, as we were 'not allowed in there'.

'Yes,' said Mam. 'You can go where you like here. This is our home.'

And my brother and I ran, whooping like Red Indians, through the house and up and down the stairs and out into the back garden until we were exhausted.

It was a particular relief for my mother to leave Dan-y-graig Terrace, because my elder sister, Joan, had died at the age of four during the time she had lived there. She fell victim to peritonitis, the result of a badly diagnosed appendicitis. I cannot remember her at all, but my mother constantly talked about her and her big dark violet blue eyes stared solemnly down on us from the enlarged photograph in its oval brown frame which hung on the wall in the front room. She was an almost tangible presence in the house until my sister Carol started to grow from a baby into a self-assertive little girl and gradually dissipated the hold that my dead sister had over my mother's mind.

It was a happy place to live in and as we were surrounded by neighbours equally new to the estate, there was no feeling of having to keep up with the Joneses – most of the families were called Jones anyway. There was a family on either side of us; the Foulkses on the left and the Johnses on the right, and we were soon borrowing from each other – a cup of sugar, 'a piece of cheese for our Joe's box'.

The geography of the estate was peculiar, to say the least. Grenfell Park House, after which the estate was named, had been demolished just after the First World War, and the council houses built on the land upon which it had stood. Grenfell Park Road ran along the side of Kilvey Hill forming the north side of the recreation ground, and St Leger Crescent swept down the hill in a slow curve, skirting St Thomas Church and meeting up with Port Tennant Road at the bottom. Pen-ys-acoed Avenue led down from Grenfell Park Road in an 'L' shape, joining up with St Leger Crescent and leaving, in the space between, a piece of spare ground which became known as 'the patch' and which was the arena for all our childhood games. We fought the Great War all over again on it, played mothers and fathers and doctors and nurses – monitored by our parents, who could look down on our activities from their bedroom windows, and hurl admonishments if and when the occasion demanded.

We were a close family, and although as we grew up Fred, Carol and I quarrelled quite a lot over trivial things, Mam and Dad never seemed to do so, and whatever happened we felt secure in the knowledge that they were always there to console us in our darkest moments and exult with us in our times of success.

My father was a dapper little man who had worked his way up from lathering customers – having to stand on an orange box to do so – in his uncle's barber shop when he was only twelve, to become a commercial traveller in the wholesale grocery firm of Walters and Batchelors in St Mary's Street, off Swansea's High Street.

He was never very well paid – I think thirty shillings a week was his salary when we were kids – so he supplemented his income by entering cartoon competitions in the *South Wales Evening Post*. These were open to all comers and had to be of a sporting nature. When he was young he had shown exceptional talent as an artist and was admitted to Swansea Art School. However, he was forced to leave after a short while because his mother wanted him to go to work to help support the family. He was so disappointed that he left all his paints and pencils behind in his desk.

He was one of seven children. Will was the eldest of the boys, then came Dad (Frederick Ernest), then Stanley, Harry and Cyril. The two girls were Josie – the eldest child – and Margery, a beautiful redhead who played the piano in Woolworth's for years, demonstrating sheet music. Everybody knew Aunty Marge – she was a stunner.

Stanley, Harry and Cyril all worked for South Wales Transport as conductors when I was a lad, their fingers stained green through handling all the coppers in those leather bags they wore across their shoulders. When they worked the

St Thomas train route I was always pleased to see them – I'd get a big wink, a joke and a free ride.

Uncle Cyril went on to be an inspector on the buses, and when I was a schoolboy he was my idol. He was always telling funny stories and was a great favourite in concerts around the town. His speciality was playing an ordinary household saw. He would place it between his legs, then, by striking the surface with a drumstick, he was able to manipulate it into making music. The sound he produced was like a high-pitched soprano – which was what he might have become had he not been careful with the lethal teeth of his instrument.

Margery's husband, George Charles, was another character who influenced me a lot in my impressionable years. He had dabbled in show business when he was a youth, and was quite a good tap dancer. Thanks to him I was able to learn a few steps myself – the result of a handful of lessons on odd Saturday mornings. However, his main claim to fame was the fact that he was the drummer with the Keskersays Dance Band which played every week at the Langland Bay Hotel. Uncle George was known to everyone locally and he and Aunty Marge were a very glamorous pair in my eyes.

Dad's mother, Nana – as we called her – was also quite 'card'. She was the life and soul of many a social gathering when she put on my grandfather's working clothes and sang the old music hall songs.

Bampa Secombe, as long as I could remember, always sat in an old upright wooden armchair near the fire, puffing away under his thick grey moustache on a smelly old pipe, with a spittoon at his feet. In his day he had been a stonemason, a trade only Will, his eldest son, had taken up after him. The poor old fellow's chest was forever rattling and I can rarely recall him standing up. He was a pretty good shot with the tobacco juice, though – something I always envied him. My juvenile attempts at emulating him at home with an impro-vised spittoon were strenuously suppressed.

George and Margery lived with my grandparents at number 38 William Street, along with their son, Freddie. He was an extremely mischievous boy who always made me laugh. He still does.

The house backed on to the Vetch Field, the home of Swansea's Football Club, and in order to watch the games the family erected a wooden stand which could only be reached by a ladder. On Saturdays the Secombe males would turn up in force for their free entertainment, and the platform would rock to and fro in rhythm with the ebb and flow of the match. It was strange to see how these gentle little men turned into red-faced militants as they yelled abuse at the referee.

As the years went by, the Swansea FC built higher and higher fences around the ground, and our family responded by increasing the height of the stand, until it got so precarious that my mother forbade me to go to William Street on a Saturday. Dad and Fred still went, but I was secretly glad not to go. Soccer never held much fascination for me, and to be perfectly honest I found the transformation of my uncles and their friends from kindly men into roaring loonies a bit frightening.

But I still remember with nostalgia the smoke-filled kitchen at number 38 after the match, where Dad and his brothers would play crib; the cries of 'fifteen one, fifteen two, fifteen four and one for his nob', and the odd juicy plop as another of Bampa's well-aimed shots found its mark.

That, very briefly, sums up my father's side of the family – and, on reflection, it seems pretty obvious how my theatrical ambitions began to take shape.

Another factor in the formation of my desire to become involved in the theatre was the time I spent as a choirboy. From the age of seven, when I first donned a cassock and surplice much too big for my diminutive size, I was hooked on the church. But although I loved the hymns and the ritual I wasn't so keen on the sermons.

St Stephen's Church in Dan-y-graig was the first church I attended as a choirboy. It was the church which my parents belonged to and was just a few yards along from where we used to live in Dan-y-graig Terrace. A small Gothic building, it stood next to the red corrugated iron Church Hall where I gave my first-ever performance. I was a cat in the Sunday School concert and wore a white cat suit with a long tail and a face mask which my father had decorated rather handsomely with whiskers and a little black nose. For the life of me I cannot remember what the play was all about, but I do know that I was the cause of tears among other members of the cast for being too hearty in my interpretation of the part – something I was to be accused of at various times in my future career. I also held up the curtain for some minutes due to the fact that I had dropped one of my cat paw gloves down the toilet, and I refused to go on until it had been dried out. It was put on a radiator – and the smell of that steaming, pee-soaked object remains with me to this day.

My tenure with the St Stephen's choir was fairly short-lived as my folks thought it was too far for Fred and me to have to walk from our house in St Leger Crescent. We transferred our allegiance to St Thomas Church, a larger building which was at the foot of our street. It was the parish church of St Thomas and could be seen for miles – a greyhound of a church looking haughtily down on the mongrel Nonconformist chapels of Port Tennant, its chimes both a reproach and a summons.

On a Sunday those bells controlled my life and Fred's. Eight o'clock communion, then eleven o'clock for the first service, Sunday School at three and six o'clock for evensong. We were up and down St Leger like little yo-yos.

The church played a vital part in Fred's life, because at the age of about twelve, after hearing one particular sermon by a missionary, he made up his mind to become a clergyman and he never at any time wavered from that decision. There was a faint hope in my mother's breast that I would feel a similar call, but after I read the lesson one Sunday morning in the distinctive tones of Sandy Powell, my favourite comedian, she abandoned the idea.

Yet I liked going to church. I would seek the mote-filled shafts of light coming through the stained-glass windows, imagining that they were spotlights and I was a tragic actor. I could hold on to an 'Amen' longer than anybody except the vicar's wife, who had a ship's siren-like quality to her voice. She was referred to rather unkindly within our family as the 'fog-horn conclusion'. The only time I would switch off the dramatic effect was during the sermon when I would surreptitiously unwrap a toffee, avoiding the watchful eye of the choirmaster, who had a mirror above the keyboard of the organ so that he could keep control of his charges. He knew better than anyone that butter would melt in my mouth – especially butterscotch. It was often a race to finish the sweet before the end of the sermon, but occasionally it was possible to get through two toffees before the sermon finished. I became rather expert at judging whether a visiting preacher would deliver a one- or two-toffee sermon, although I was once badly caught out by a missionary from Uganda who finished so abruptly I inhaled a pear drop – an event which brought a gleam of satisfaction to the reflected eye of our choirmaster.

Despite my theatrical aspirations I was really terribly shy and whenever I had a solo to sing it felt like torture. My mouth would go dry and my voice would take on a wobble which threatened to burst the seams of my mother's gloves as she gripped the back of the pew in front of her.

This shyness attacked me even when I was invited to sing within the family circle. Every Sunday after church we all went along to my mother's parents in Jersey Terrace, which was off Dan-y-graig Road, opposite the cemetery. Aunty Doris, who was married to Mam's brother Tom, would bang away on the battered old upright piano and various members of the family would do their party pieces. My father was always called upon to do 'The Wreck of the 11.69', a parody of 'The Wreck of the Hesperus', which he could only perform if he had a chair to hold on to. Mam would sing something in her contralto and Grandad

Davies, who had been a bass soloist in Anglesey Cathedral, would contribute 'Heigh-ho said Anthony Rowley' or something from Gilbert and Sullivan. My sister, Carol, who was the star of the Secombe family, would do some acrobatics or a comedy monologue – and then it would be my turn.

Because I was so shy, it became standard procedure for me to go to the outside toilet and leave the door open to allow my audience to listen from inside the kitchen. I would perch on the wooden seat, my trousers around my ankles – the squares of newspaper hanging from a nail on the wall my only set decoration – and launch into 'Rock of Ages' or 'Abide with Me', accompanied fitfully by the odd tomcat. It was fine in the summer evenings, but the wind off the sea in the winter was pretty cruel, and sometimes even today when I sing those hymns goose-pimples form in the most odd places.

My grandfather on Mam's side, Thomas Arthur Davies, was a very interesting character. He was born out of wedlock to a young lady in the village of Clun in Shropshire. She refused to marry his father, the son of a local landowner. His education was taken over by the village parson, and my grandfather turned out to be a very bright pupil, but owing to his illegitimacy he was denied entry to the professions. Eventually he became a teacher on board the *Clio*, a training ship for young delinquents which was permanently anchored in the Conway Strait.

He met my grandmother, Caroline, when she was sixteen, and they eloped. She was the daughter of a yeoman farmer called Edwards who had been killed in a hunting accident, leaving his children £2,000 each in his will. With her endowment they bought a small hotel near Bristol on a bank of the River Severn. Unfortunately he was not properly insured, and one day the Severn Bore, the tidal wave which sweeps periodically up the estuary, was higher than usual and the

> *Life is mostly froth & bubble.*
> *Two things stand like stone.*
> *Kindness is in another's trouble*
> *Courage in one's own.*
>
> *Money lost. much lost;*
> *Honour lost. most lost;*
> *Courage lost, all lost.*
>
> Swansea
> Aug 16·1935
> / "

hotel was flooded. They lost everything and had to be rescued by rowing boat from the bedroom.

After that he had a variety of jobs, none of which were commensurate with his intelligence and he took to drinking heavily. By the time I became aware of his history he was working as a tallyman on the docks, credited with having the finest copperplate handwriting anyone had ever seen in that particular job.

Like Bampa Secombe, he too sat for hours in his wooden chair by the fire in the living-room of the terraced house in Jersey Terrace. He had an uncertain temper, but he was good company for Fred and myself when he'd had a flagon or two. He encouraged us to read good books, and by the time my brother was about ten, Grandpa Davies had taken him through Gibbon's *Decline and Fall of the Roman Empire*. Fred was the apple of his eye because he could see his potential. He wasn't so sure about me. I was never still long enough for him to get to know me properly. Then, when I was seven, both Fred and I contracted scarlet fever and were taken to the Isolation Hospital. Life was very restricted in there and I was forced to lie in my bed and read. Grandad sent me all of Sir Walter Scott's 'Waverley' novels as a present, and I devoured them eagerly. The print was very small, and by the time I was released from hospital I was permanently short-sighted – but I could recite Sir Walter's prose by the yard.

My grandmother suffered from an extreme case of rheumatoid arthritis and was bent like a bow from the waist. In spite of this she was always busy around the house. I can see her now in her black buttoned boots and black bombazine dress and white apron, her hair – of which she was very proud – piled high in a bun, as she whistled away. She had no teeth, but she could whistle like a man. The big copper in which she did the washing was, in season, the vat in which she made her elderberry or parsnip wine, and many a Pearl Insurance man or rent collector would reel down the steps after a couple of glasses of her brew.

There was always a copy of *The Tatler* on the oil-clothed table, and Gran knew the names of all the royalty in Europe and all the spicier bits of gossip about the elegant folk who always seemed to be photographed opened-mouthed with forks of food poised for ingestion. She would grin wickedly as she tapped her crooked finger at a photograph of some high-born lady and say ''Er was a proper little tart in 'er time.' And she could quell her husband into submission with a stern 'Tom, behave yourself.'

Mam had two sisters and two brothers – Doll and May, and Harry and Tom. Tom was married to Aunty Doris, whom I have already mentioned, and Harry was married to Essie – more of them later. Aunty Doll was the youngest of the Davies children and my mother, Nellie Jane Gladys, was the eldest. Aunty May was the manageress of Peacock's Bazaar in

Swansea Market (a position once held by my mother) until, after a long engagement, she married Maudsley Adams.

They conducted their courtship in the front parlour in Jersey Terrace – a room which was always tidy and smelt of mothballs. It was only used on Sundays because the piano was in there, otherwise it was reserved for receiving the insurance man on paying out days and for May and Maudsley's lengthy wooing. Maudsley had an artificial leg and when we saw his stick in the hallway we kids would tiptoe past the parlour down to the kitchen, trying to suppress our giggles.

Saturdays were special days for me because I was allowed to go with my mother into town on the tram to do the shopping in Swansea. My task was to help carry home the carrier bags up the steep hill from the tram stop. My reward for doing this was a fish and chip supper at the Dolphin behind the market, or faggots and peas in the market itself.

It was like Aladdin's cave in the Market for a young boy. Football boots hung from the canopies of leather-wear stalls and the confectionery stalls held veritable mountains of pear drops, boiled sweets in the shape of goldfish – which if put in your mouth sideways gave you a sticky grin from ear to ear – coconut mushrooms, liquorice allsorts of every conceivable hue, and trays of toffee which had to be broken with a silver hammer. There were bookstalls, which were always a great attraction for me, especially at Christmas time when all the boys' annuals came out. *The Wizard, The Rover, The Magnet, The Champion* – all these comics had a hardback edition published in time for the festive season. There was the stall where Mam would buy laverbread for our regular Sunday breakfast of laverbread, bacon and fried bread. Lots of people knew my mother, and she loved a good gossip. I would hop from foot to foot as I waited for her to move on to the next piece of scandal, the string handles of the carrier bags beginning to dig into my fingers.

'Come on, Mam,' I'd wheedle. But she was never one to be hurried along.

'I waited nine months for you, so you can wait five minutes for me,' was her standard reply.

But there was never anything to compare with the utter bliss and contentment I felt sitting with her at a table in the crowded Dolphin, the fruits of our shopping resting against our chairs, and the steam from a fourpenny hake cutlet and threepenny-worth of lovely fat chips clouding my spectacles.

'There's a good boy, now, eat up tidy.'

And I would, oh I would.

My father seldom came shopping with us because he couldn't stand the crowds. During the First World War he had been blown up by a shell in the Battle of Neuve Chapelle and he was the recipient of a war pension, which I always collected for him from the post office in Port Tennant Road. I usually did the messages for the household, a chore I was quite happy with because it gave me a legitimate reason for running.

I ran everywhere. I ran to school, I ran to choir practice, I ran to Sunday School, I ran to the grocer's, the butcher's, the post office, and I ran into Swansea to my father's place of work, Walters and Batchelors, with my father's 'book'. This last trip was always worth threepence because it entailed a long jog and was pretty important. The 'book' was a black, ruled notebook containing the orders, written in beautiful copperplate, that my father had taken on his perambulations around the little grocery shops in the Swansea Valleys. It also contained the money he had collected, all wrapped around with rubber bands. My job was to take the 'book' and post it in the letter-box, make sure it dropped, and then come home. The money made it a pretty dangerous operation in my young mind, and I used to see myself as a Pony Express rider taking the US Mail through Indian territory.

Down St Leger Crescent I would lope, my gym shoes squeaking on the pavements; past the church, down on to

Port Tennant Road – head moving from side to side for signs of trouble – skipping the piles of dog turds, skidding around the corner by East Dock station; and if by some mischance the New Cut Bridge had opened to allow a ship to go through, I'd mark time on the spot until it closed, then off I'd go again, a horseless Buffalo Bill carrying at least eight pounds in notes and silver.

After the long pull up Wind Street it was only a few yards down the narrow St Mary's Street to my destination. Once the 'book' had thudded safely through the brass letter-box I would turn around and head for home, still running, but this time I would be the Last of the Mohicans – fleet of foot, looking for tracks in the snow. Once, running in the gutter, eagle-eyed for any signs of grizzly bears, I came across a threepenny bit outside a pub at the bottom of Wind Street. Immediately I became a hazard to trams and cyclists as I ran, head down, looking for loose change. I picked up about three more coins that evening, and, though from that day on I never found any more money, it took innumerable collisions with lamp-posts and prostrate drunken seamen before I could persuade myself to leave the gutter to those who lived there and get back to running on the pavement. I suppose you could say that I had a good run for my father's money.

My constant companion, from the time I was about five or six right up to the time I passed the scholarship and went to Dynevor Secondary School, was Ronnie Jones. His house was a few doors away in Grenfell Park Road and he lived there with his mother and father. Mr Jones was the captain of a tug boat and was the image of Spencer Tracy – or he would have been if he'd had any teeth. Ronnie's mother was a small lady who always smelt of apples with a slight hint of gin.

Ronnie had been born with a cleft palate which made his speech difficult to understand when he was young, and I was the only one who could make out what he was saying. So when he was sent on an errand I used to go with him as a sort of interpreter. It worked pretty well as a rule, although things went rather badly wrong one Saturday lunchtime. Mrs Jones sent us to the butcher's to get half a pound of steak and a pound of sausages, and we were given twopence each for going. Unfortunately, on the way to the shop we got so involved in trying to decide what to do with our money that we arrived before Mr Allchurch, the straw-boatered butcher, uncertain whether it was a pound of steak and a half a pound of sausages or vice versa. Eventually we decided on the former, not realizing that the difference in price was considerable in those days, and anyway it was to be charged.

When we got back to Mrs Jones, we found her half-way up the stairs. Ronnie handed her his purchases through the banisters. She opened the parcel containing the pound of steak, and saw the cost of her house-keeping soaring. A lady with a volatile temper, she proceeded to lose it at once, and with an ear-splitting screech she hurled the steak at Ronnie, who ducked, and the man from the Pearl – who had followed us over the threshold – took it full in the face. The steak fell to the floor, where the next-door neighbour's cat, which had been sunning itself on the back doorstep, smartly fielded it and, unable to believe its luck, promptly disappeared into the wilderness which was the Bayless's garden.

Ronnie and I went our separate ways when we reached the age of twelve or thereabouts, but we always remained good chums. It was part of our childhood dreams together that we would one day go hunting lions in Africa. Many years later, when the news came out in the *South Wales Evening Post* that my regiment, the Swansea TA Artillery, had participated in the North African landings, Ronnie met my mother at a bus stop in town. He tapped her on the shoulder with his paper and said, 'He's gone to Africa without me, after all.' And his eyes were bright with tears.

Some of the happiest days of my childhood were spent with my Uncle Harry and Aunty Essie in Llangyfelach. Harry

Davies was my mother's brother and I was named after him. He came to see my mother just after I was born and said, 'If that little bugger is not christened Harry after me, I'll never talk to you again.'

And Harry I became – Harry Donald Secombe. The 'Donald' was my father's idea. He firmly believed that his ancestors came from Scotland – although subsequently we discovered that his family originated from Cornwall. So much for ancestry.

Uncle Harry was an indomitable character. He had lost an eye in the First World War and wore a glass replica with which he played stomach-churning practical jokes. When he played cricket with us he would take off his coat to serve as a wicket, and put his glass eye on it, saying, 'Now, keep your eye on the ball.' He was not averse to dropping it in the fruit salad at tea-time and serving it up to a visitor if he thought he or she needed a laugh.

Aunty Essie was very jolly, very fat and always laughing. She spoiled Carol and Fred and me whenever we stayed there for weekends. The rivalry between us used to be intense, and it was always a matter for tears for the two who were left behind – only one of us could be accommodated at a time. Margaret was their only child, and she was always looked upon by us as a sister. We were all envious of her in a way. She could swim extremely well, ride like a cowboy and outrun us all.

They lived on Llangyfelach Common, a few miles from Morriston, and to me it was Shangri-La. I would get the bus from Christina Street after school on Friday and sit on the top deck, nursing my school satchel which contained a change of clothes for the weekend, and urging the driver to go faster. When the bus stopped at the Plough and Harrow in Llangyfelach, Uncle Harry and Margaret would be there to meet me and away we'd go, whooping and yelling across the common.

There was no electricity in the house for the first years I can remember, and I used to love the smell of the paraffin lamps which provided illumination for each room. The house was redolent with good smells – pipe smoke, bacon frying in the morning, machine oil from Uncle Harry's motorbike and sidecar, and the sweet scent of hay from the stable where Grandpa Cranfield, Aunty Essie's father, kept his horse and cart. There was also the smell of horse manure, which was not all that pleasant and which I invariably brought in on my shoes from the yard.

'Take those bloody shoes off before you come in here, you little bugger, you!' Uncle Harry never minced his words, but he never meant anything unkindly.

Saturday was the day Margaret and I would go out with Grandpa Cranfield in his horse-drawn cart delivering blocks of fuel. I loved that – a good excuse for getting absolutely black without fear of recrimination. The old man was quite a character. He came from Oxfordshire and looked the proper countryman with his knee-high leggings and stout boots, and the eternal hand-rolled cigarette dyeing his straggly grey moustache with nicotine. I used to watch him groom Amy the horse, named after Amy Johnson the celebrated flier. He would hiss away between his teeth as he curry-combed her till she shone. I was allowed to sit on her back and trot around the yard, but I never really got the hang of it – not like Margaret, who could ride bareback like an Apache.

Llangyfelach was where I learned to do important things, like how to tie my shoe laces properly, how to get a proper knot in my school tie, and how to ride a bike. There was love in abundance in that little house on the common, and I always shed a tear when the time came to leave. But life had to go on and school loomed large on Monday mornings.

CHAPTER TWO

Schooldays – Could Do Better

The first school the three of us attended was St Thomas' Infants. It was part of a large, red-brick, educational sandwich – Infants at the bottom, Boys in the middle and Girls on the top floor. I took to school very well in the beginning. My mother had taken me along with her for company when Fred was enrolled, and to her surprise I didn't want to go home. Carol, though, after her first day at school refused to go back on the second day, saying firmly, 'I've left.'

Playtime was my favourite subject, although the hard asphalt of the playground made contact sports hazardous. I fell down one day and cut my knee rather badly. Miss Leonard, the headmistress, carried me into her office and gave me a glass of pop and a biscuit with an iced butterfly on top. For several weeks after that incident I kept falling down outside her office, but I never got another biscuit.

The games we enjoyed in those days seem all to have disappeared. We played marbles – where you placed a number of marbles inside a chalked circle and then in turn tried to knock them out of the ring with a glass alley from the top of a lemonade bottle, or a steel ball if you were lucky enough to have one. The horse chestnut season brought with it the game of conkers, in which you threaded a piece of string through a conker and set out in search of someone else with a similar weapon. You would then hold your conker still on the end of

The Angel

An angel came to me
at night.

He was clad in a robe of
shimmering white:

The plaited locks hung
down his back:

His handsome face did
nothing lack:

He carried in his hand
a book of gold,

With the names of persons,
young and old,

Who were to go to realms
above

Where angels call
good Lord "Love."

By Harry Secombe. Aged 11.
  7 St. Leger Crescent,
    St. Thomas,
      Swansea.
      Glamorgan

its string so that your opponent could take a whack at it. If it survived, you then had a turn at demolishing his conker. Each conker you destroyed was then added to your score, provided yours stayed intact. 'Conker six', for example, meant that your conker had seen off six others. I was never very good at that game – either my chestnut shattered at the first go or it flew off the string when I aimed it at an adversary.

I could whip a pretty good top, though. These were wooden mushroom-shaped pegs, gaily striped, which you spun on the ground with the aid of a string whip. Great stuff.

As the years went by I progressed from the Infants' School and into the Boys' section. I was a dunce in anything to do with mathematics, but I did rather well in English composition and drawing.

There was a temporary set-back in my education when I contracted scarlet fever, because, as I related earlier, my eyesight had been affected by an overdose of Sir Walter Scott. I was not aware of how bad my eyes were until I returned to Mr Minty's class following my illness. I was placed at the back of the classroom and found that I was unable to read what he wrote on the blackboard, with the result that I got caned for being stupid. After this had happened a couple of times I came home crying one lunchtime and complained to my father, who happened to be home that day. He was furious – something that rarely happened, in my experience – and insisted on coming back to see 'Mr McGinty', as he called him. I don't know what he said to him, but Mr Minty put me in the front row that afternoon and never again laid a hand on me.

The result of the confrontation was that my parents realized something had to be done about my eyesight, and I went along to the clinic for a test. I was found to be extremely myopic and, in due course, I was given a pair of glasses. The difference was literally staggering. I could see so much more with them on that I almost fell down when I left the optician's. I could read the names of the shops, I could see Kilvey Hill clearly and not as a grey blur, and I didn't care if the whole world called me 'old four-eyes'– I could see!

The next milestone of my school days came when I reached the scholarship class. This was taught by Mr Corfield, a fine teacher in his late forties who knew how to encourage boys to do their best. Mr Corfield took a liking to the way I wrote my essays and showed me how to construct a sentence properly, but he realized, along with every other teacher I had, that maths was a closed book to me.

'Never mind, Secombe,' he'd say. 'One day you'll be a writer.'

Years later when I was topping the bill at the Palladium, I was visiting my folks in Swansea when I heard that Mr Corfield was not too well. I went along to see him, exhibiting all the trappings of showbiz success – the Rolex watch, the snappy suit and the big car. He was well wrapped up and sitting by the fire when I entered his house.

'Hello, Mr Corfield,' I bellowed over-heartily.

He looked at me for some thirty seconds and then said, 'Harry, what went wrong?'

A preliminary examination was held each year before the scholarship proper, and the first time I sat it I passed, much to everyone's surprise, as I was really too young for the main exam, which I failed.

The next year I passed both examinations and elected to go to Dynevor Secondary School, principally because my brother, Fred, was already there and I would have company on the way to school. I don't think Fred was all that keen on the idea, because I was getting to be a bit of a handful. He was also nearly three years older than me, a huge gap when you're young. However, I was very proud of my school cap and tie which I wore with an ordinary jacket; Mam's budget didn't allow for a blazer. 'Nihil sine labore' was the motto emblazoned on the cap – 'Nothing without work' – ominous words, I thought.

Dynevor was a school where the emphasis was on learning, and it provided a good pre-university education for boys like Fred, who was clearly destined for an academic career. For me, it was like stepping into the world of *The Magnet* with Harry Wharton and his pals. The masters wore gowns, and we had a school orchestra, cricket nets, a fives court – all brand new experiences for me. Chaps played pranks on the masters just as the Greyfriars boys did in my favourite comic.

I chose to take French and German rather than Welsh and German, and was put in the 'A' stream. This turned out to be somewhat unfortunate for me because my brother was also an 'A' pupil, and every master reminded me of how well he had done before me.

'Hope you're as good as your brother,' they'd say, patting me heavily on the head with some weighty tome.

But, of course, I never was – except in English and art. When the exam results came out I would be 29th in arithmetic,

REPORT for ___Easter___ Term ending ___Jan___ 19 36

Name ___Secombe H.D.___ Form ___4a___

Age 14 yrs 2 mths. Height 5 ft 0 ins. Weight 6 st 11½ lbs.

Average Age of Form 14·7 No. of Boys in Form 32 Position 27

Subject.	Maximum	Marks	Position	Remarks	Subject.	Maximum	Marks	Position	Remarks
ENGLISH Comp Gram	50 100	30 50	4 15	S S	ARITHMETIC	50	3	31	P ✗
do. Literature	100	44	11	JS	ALGEBRA	100	41	25	V.7
GEOGRAPHY I.	200	58	21	WK ✗	GEOMETRY	100	0	31	V.P. ✗
do. II.					MATHEMATICS I.				
HISTORY	200	92	14	V.7	do. II.				
do. European					CHEMISTRY I.	150	17	31	P. ✗
FRENCH	200	91	23	V.7	do. II.	50	40	14	S
do. Literature					PHYSICS I.	150	34	30	V.P
GERMAN	200	66	19	P. ✗	do. II.	50	38	21	S
do. Literature					ART	100	68	9	VS.
WELSH					WOODWORK	100	⁄	⁄	⁄
do. Literature			37% (circled)		METAL WORK	100	30	11	WK. ✗
LATIN					MUSIC	100	⁄	⁄	⁄
do. Literature									
GREEK									

Absent ___8___ half-days. Late ___0___ times. House Marks: Gained ___0___ Lost ___1___

School Activities ___School Choir · 1st Prize Short Story.___

Conduct ___G___

Remarks: ___A very disappointing result from a capable lad. There must be a greater striving for accuracy.___

Form Master ___G. Birrell___

___Determined effort is necessary. The Art shows a falling off in his work.___

Head Master, ___Llewelyn John___ A.R.C.S., B.Sc.

Parent or Guardian ___F. E. Secombe___ (Signed)

Remark _____

Next Term begins on _____

31st in algebra and 1st in English and art. 'Could do better' was the theme of every housemaster's end-of-term summary of my efforts.

Every year we had a school Eisteddfod, and for some reason I decided in my first term in school to enter in the poetry recitation section. The poem we all had to learn was W H Davies's 'Can I forget the sweet days that have been?' I declaimed the damned thing all over the house – I even recited it to the milkman one morning.

'Very nice,' he said, with an utter lack of conviction. Behind him his horse removed three feet of privet from the hedge next door.

I must have bored half the street with my treble-registered interpretation of the Welsh tramp poet's masterpiece.

Then came the day of the eisteddfod and the moment I had been looking forward to. The whole school was assembled in the Hall, and when my name was announced I stood up to begin the walk up on to the platform where the judges sat awaiting my efforts. Suddenly I realized what I had let myself in for, and my knees began to do castanet impressions. My glasses misted over and I stumbled up the steps, vaguely aware of the forbidding presence of Mr 'Beak' John, the headmaster (so-called because of his large nose), sitting in his chair drumming his fingers impatiently.

'Can I forget the sweet days that have been,' I began, dry-mouthed and even higher-pitched than usual. Then the words flew from my mind and I stood, petrified, looking at the mass of faces before me. I tried again. 'Can I forget the sweet days that have been,' and still nothing came. I repeated the line three more times and then, mercifully, my brother Fred, who was near the front as an on-duty prefect, came up on to the rostrum and led me off, still babbling that traumatic first line.

That experience has never left me, and sometimes on first nights it comes into the back of my mind and a little *frisson* of fear starts up the spine.

*

Despite this débâcle I still had a vague desire to do something in the theatre. I had become a rabid wireless fanatic; indeed the whole family had become 'hooked'. Dad had hired a Rediffusion set with that familiar rising sun motif on the loudspeaker and three stations to choose from – BBC Home, BBC Light and Radio Luxembourg, which was the commercial station with all the advertising jingles. 'We are the Ovaltinies', 'Hurrah for Beetox, what a delightful smell, the stuff that every self-respecting grocer has to sell,' etc. These were tunes that we kids sang ad nauseam. Pre-Rediffusion, Dad had been given an old crystal set which seemed to work very fitfully.

'I've got it!' he would cry as he twiddled the crystal, then 'Damn and blast!' He'd lost it again.

Now we had the world at our command. I don't think we ever missed 'Saturday Night Music Hall' and 'In Town Tonight'. The comedians were my favourites – Rob Wilton, Stanley Holloway with his monologues about 'The Lion and Albert' and 'Sam, Pick Oop Tha' Musket', Sandy Powell, Tommy Handley, Suzette Tarry with her signature tune, 'Red Sails in the Sunset', and – everybody's favourite – Gracie Fields. I loved them all. Billy Bennett, Scott and Waley, Bennett and Williams with their 'phono-fiddles', Clapham and Dwyer, Max Miller and Flanagan and Allen were like intimate friends.

On the way to school I used to pass the poster on the wall of Weaver's Flour Mills, which revealed who was appearing at the Swansea Empire each week, and I would almost swoon with the knowledge that one of my favourites was actually in the same town as me, breathing the same air. I would haunt the back of the Empire hoping for just a glimpse of one of my heroes. George Charles, who knew the stage door-keeper, used to leave my autograph book with him for the stars to sign, and I would pore for hours over the famous names. That's the reason why I never mind signing autographs today – they mean such a lot to some kids. One of my great disappointments was to discover that Roy Fox, the bandleader, had not really signed my book at all, but had used a rubber stamp. That shook my faith in human nature.

My daily intake of radio comedy began to manifest itself in impersonations of my idols, until eventually I had a whole repertoire which I used to trot out on family get-togethers.

Another influence on me was the local cinema, which went through various transformations in my boyhood. At first it was called the Pictorium, or the 'Pic', and then it was refurbished and became the Scala, a name we kids could never pronounce properly. It was the dream factory for the neighbourhood and stood at the confluence of two roads, Foxhole and Morris Lane, a very steep hill which led to the council estate. We would come roaring down the lane on a Saturday afternoon, Ronnie Jones and I, to join the queue for the 'twopenny rush'. The first task was to buy sweets to take in with us from the little sweet shop at the bottom of Morris Lane. There we were faced with an agonizing choice. A sherbet dab? A lucky packet? (This usually contained fibrous twigs of raw liquorice and tiger nuts.) Or a pennorth of unshelled peanuts? I usually plumped for a bullseye, which would at least last most of the main feature, although there would not be the satisfaction of watching it change colour when the lights went out.

Inside the cinema the smell of wet knickers, orange peel and carbolic flowed over us like a warm, sticky bath and the ravaged plush seats held all sorts of perils – old chewing gum underneath, and the odd stain from a previous tenant's over-excitement. The din before the lights went out was indescribable, and sometimes the manager in his boiled shirt and dickie bow would come out in front of the curtains and threaten us with mass expulsion if we didn't calm down. This normally did the trick, and the curtains would eventually jerk back and the projectors would clatter into life, and a collective sigh would go up as the titles appeared on the screen.

Cowboy films and African jungle epics were my favourites when I was very small, and then I progressed to a fondness for 'Andy Hardy' and gangster films. When the exit doors were flung open – always before the end of the serial, so that the screen became blank – I would emerge from the cinema as James Cagney or Mickey Rooney. All the way back up the hill I'd be reliving the film, firing imaginary bullets at unheeding old ladies behind their lace curtains in Morris Lane, or swinging precariously from the lower limb of the dead tree at the end of Grenfell Park Road. My parents never knew who would come home from the pictures on a Saturday afternoon.

Sometimes at the evening performances children were allowed in with an adult, because in those days there were no 'X' rated films. Mam and Dad rarely went to the the 'Pic'; Dad because he'd have to leave half-way through the performance with an attack of hyperventilation, and Mam because she preferred going to the Plaza on a Wednesday afternoon with her friend, Mrs Beynon, who live opposite us in Pen-ys-acoed Avenue.

However, there was one person who was always good-natured enough to take other people's children with her on these occasions. Her name was Mrs Bayless, and she lived a couple of doors up from our house at the top of St Leger Crescent. She came from the Midlands and had about six children of her own. Thus, when we all trooped up the step behind her, she would demand one ticket for herself and sometimes as many as twelve half-price tickets would spew out of the machine in the booth for the rest of us. The manager, unable to do anything about it, would tear the stubs in half with controlled fury and pass us through into the cinema. In the evenings it was a completely different place from the scene of the 'twopenny rush' – discreet organ music would be playing and an overpowering perfumed disinfectant concealed the unspeakable odours of the matinée.

Mrs Bayless also exchanged ladies' magazines with my mother – publications like *True Story* and *Confessions* which Mam used to hide from us. I found the hiding-place one day on top of the wardrobe in her bedroom and became hooked on the delicious dots which always came at the end of a steamy passage, where the reader was left to his or her imagination – a quality I had in abundance. The readers' page always intrigued me – even though the problems that 'Worried of Walthamstow' or 'Distraught of Denbigh' were seeking advice about were beyond the experience of a spotty, bespectacled twelve-year-old. A bucket of cold water would have done us all the world of good.

This was the time when I was becoming aware of girls, although I was pretty shy in their company. There was one particular girl I took a tongue-tied fancy to, by the name of Enid Passmore. Her parents kept a fruiterer's shop near the cinema and I used to see her on the way home from school. She went to Delabeche, which was the sister school to Dynevor, and I was sometimes allowed to carry her books home. She was a strapping brunette with a ready grin which revealed one slightly chipped front tooth. She treated me with a teasing condescension and I never at any time spent even five minutes alone in her company. But her black wool stockings and her toothy smile haunted my boyhood dreams for many a month.

The first romance I ever had was with a very pretty little girl called Mildred O'Malley. She lived in Pen-ys-acoed with her brothers and parents, and her father was the proud owner of a three-wheel Morgan runabout. I must have been about ten when we got married.

The event took place on 'the patch', the piece of waste ground on the estate which looked as if it was the result of the architect having left a packet of cigarettes on the blueprint and absent-mindedly drawn around it.

It was a warm Saturday afternoon and a tent had been set up for the wedding. Joyce Griffiths, who was a bit older than me, was the parson, wearing one of her father's collars back to front and armed, for some reason, with an umbrella. The bride was all ready with her white dress, a lace doily as a veil and a bunch of buttercups and dandelions as a bouquet.

Unfortunately, the bridegroom, Billy Beynon, had been hauled off to go shopping with his mother and so, until I happened to pass by – on the way to Mrs Gorman's sweet shop, which she had set up illegally in her front room – the wedding had come to a standstill.

'Come on, you'll do,' cried Joyce good-naturedly, and in no time I found myself standing alongside Mildred, whom I had always worshipped from a discreet distance.

Joyce rammed an old trilby on my head, reducing my vision considerably. 'Do you take this woman to be your lawful wedded wife?' she asked, pretending to read from a railway timetable.

I nodded nervously, causing the trilby to slip further down over my nose.

'Say "yes", mun,' hissed the parson.

'Yes,' I croaked.

Mildred's reply to her question was firm. 'Yeth,' she declared, bending down to pick at a scab on her knee.

'I now announce you man and wife,' said Joyce, closing the book. 'Now kiss the bride.'

My heart thumped as I turned to my new bride and pursed my lips.

'You look stupid with that hat on,' giggled Mildred.

'Go on, kiss him.' Joyce was getting a bit fed up with the whole thing.

'He's all sweaty,' Mildred observed as I removed the hat. '*Ach y fi!*'

I rubbed my face vigorously with the sleeve of my jumper and puckered up again.

'Not on the lips, you'll spoil my lipstick. My cheek.'

'Old cissy, playing with the girls!' Ronnie Jones appeared at his gate.

I blushed crimson. Before me Mildred had her eyes shut and was waiting resignedly for a kiss.

'Hurry up.' This was Joyce.

I threw the hat on the ground and kicked the wicket stump that formed the pole of the tent. 'I'm not playing any more

– it's daft,' I cried, and walked away without kissing the smooth, cold-creamed cheek that awaited me. 'Anyway, I'm sweating because I haven't been well, so there.'

That was true. I was just getting over a severe bowel infection I had picked up through eating infected ice-cream bought from a street vendor. I had been too ill to go to hospital and so Mam looked after me at home, supervised by Doctor Hefferman, who had brought me into the world. At one stage during my illness I slipped into a coma.

'This is it,' said the doctor. 'If he comes out of this he'll be all right, if he doesn't. . .' he shrugged his shoulders.

I was swathed in cold compresses to bring down my temperature which had reached 105 degrees Fahrenheit, and then they just had to wait and see. After an agonizing time for my family I slowly opened my eyes and the first thing I said, according to my mother, was 'Where's my medals?'

Apparently, to keep me quiet, my father had pinned his war medals on my pyjama jacket.

From that time on I was regarded as the 'delicate' one of the family – always prey to whatever ailment happened to be visiting the neighbourhood. I had already had scarlet fever at seven; chicken-pox was followed by German measles, followed by yellow jaundice. I think it's safe to say that I had a pretty colourful childhood.

Every summer when we were small my father took his holidays with his cousins in Cardiganshire, in a little place called Llechryd. Gran and Grandpa Bloom – we seemed to call anyone over a certain age 'Gran or Grandpa' – lived on a farm there, and were utterly self-sufficient. They had a farmhouse, a bakery, a watermill, pig sties, chickens, cattle and wheat fields. So they grew their own wheat, churned their own butter from their own cows' milk, ground their own grain in the mill, and from the flour made delicious bread.

It was a glorious place for children, and we were always made very welcome. Legs of ham hung from hooks in the kitchen ceiling, and when we came down for breakfast, old Gran Bloom, who spoke only a few words of English, would take one down, cut lovely big slices off it and throw them in a big frying pan along with some fresh eggs. What a wonderful start to the day.

Gran Bloom was Welsh-speaking, and was Dad's cousin. Her husband was of Norwegian descent, and apart from being a farmer he was also a great horticulturist. In the big orchard at the side of the farmhouse he grew huge pears, and at the end of the holiday he always gave us some to take home. He was also the proud owner of an open-topped Sunbeam tourer, in which he and his daughter Sally would drive us to Aberayron on the Cardiganshire coast for a picnic by the sea.

Because I was always recovering from, or about to have a fresh outbreak of some childhood 'crut', I rarely ventured further out into the briny than knee-deep. Mam and the other ladies would tuck their frocks into their bloomers and have a good old paddle, then get back to the car to unpack the hamper for the picnic.

Golden days indeed, and the wrench of leaving was almost too much to bear. We'd say goodbye to the chickens, the pigs, the horses, and the dogs, and I'd promise never again to climb on the bakehouse roof or let the cows out, or try to start the car, as long as I could come back again next year, please Gran. And she'd give us all a big hug and promise us it would be all right.

When we got back home I used to sit on the front gate facing Town Hill, because I knew that was west, and that's where Llechryd lay, towards the setting sun – and I'd close my eyes tightly in an effort to bring back the sights and sounds of the holiday. Then Ronnie Jones would throw a stone at me and I'd be off over to the patch to join the other kids for a game of football or 'mothers and fathers' or whatever was going on.

*

After my disastrous appearance at the school Eisteddfod, it was some time before I could bring myself to attempt anything of a similar nature except within the family circle. In fact it was a couple of years before I was recruited by Carol to perform a double act with her at a social. She was pretty well established on the local amateur concert party circuit by this time, doing funny monologues, and Mam thought it would be a good idea if the pair of us teamed up to do a comedy act. What she had in mind was a piece of material which had been recorded on a 78 rpm record by a Welsh double act called Ted and May Hopkins, who had achieved some success on the music halls in the Twenties. The record was called 'The Welsh Courtship', and as far as I can now remember it entailed me being a straight man to Carol's comic character.

We first performed it at the Central Hall in Swansea and I was in a fair old state before the performance. I couldn't bear to look at all the faces I saw out front when I peeped through the curtains before we went on, so I took my glasses off. To my great surprise I lost a lot of my nervousness when we made our entrance. The fact that I could see no individuals, only a pink sea of unidentifiable faces before me, calmed my nerves. As far as I was concerned I was just doing a 'turn' for the family at home, and when the first laughs came I revelled in them. I had found the secret of success, I thought – until I fell down the steps in the dark as we came off stage.

It's true, though, that from that day on, I was never as terrified about facing an audience again – just as long as I could not see them. The only time I ever wore glasses on stage was when I appeared in *Pickwick* over thirty years later, and that was only because the part required me to wear them.

Back at school I managed to go from form to form without distinguishing myself academically and I was never much good at sport, either – except for one occasion when I succeeded in scoring a goal in a soccer match.

We were playing on the school playing fields which were at the top of Townhill and I was wearing a pair of football boots with studs. These studs had been nailed in by my father, who, in one of his drives for home economy, had bought a cobbler's last and announced that he would do all the shoe repairs in future. (It turned out to be pretty false economy, because when it rained my soles and uppers parted company as I walked home from school, prompting the neighbours to ask, 'What kind of complaint has your Harry come down with now – him limping so badly?') On this particular day the nails were coming through into my heels every time I ran after the ball and I had adopted a watchful crouch back near the goal-keeper in the faint hope that the games master would not notice. He did.

'You're not in the slips, Secombe. This is soccer, not cricket.'

I hopped forward, trying to look keen, and received a blow in the face with the muddy ball which broke one of the arms of my spectacles. I was sent in to the changing-room to try to fix them, but there was no way I could get the arm back on again. I gave up after ten minutes, put my specs in my coat pocket and limped back on to the field, peering short-sightedly at the action before me. Suddenly the ball was at my feet and I began to dribble as well as I was able, waiting for it to be taken from me at any second. To my surprise I was able to waltz through the blurred opposition and from about ten feet from the goal, painfully booted the ball into the net. I turned, waiting for acclamation.

'You're an idiot, Secombe,' said Mr Burgess, the games master. 'We changed sides five minutes ago.'

There were little triumphs, now and again, to counterbalance my inadequacies. As, for example, when I was picked for the school choir. Mr Beynon, the music teacher, was very keen on getting together a big concert at the newly opened Brangwyn Hall, and he held auditions throughout the school for a gala performance of 'The Revenge', Tennyson's poem about Sir Richard Grenville set to music. We were also to learn 'The Blue Danube' waltz to which special lyrics had been written.

It was the first time I had had any experience of a really big occasion in a proper concert hall with a professional orchestra, and I loved it. There's a wonderful feeling when you're riding on the crest of the music, exulting in the power of communal effort, and giving the conductor your maximum attention.

We had such a tremendous reception from the audience that we sang 'The Blue Danube' three times and Mr Beynon was beside himself with pride, running up and down our serried ranks, patting our heads, beaming hugely. Just to be a small part of such success was like a heady drug, and once I had tasted it I was an addict.

Another lift to my ego was having a short story accepted for the school magazine. The sight of my effort in print almost turned my ambition away from the stage to a life of letters, and I took to leaping around the house, in what I thought was a balletic style, to records on our wind-up gramophone. I started to read poetry, and sat for ages in our back garden contemplating the weeds. My parents began to exchange worried glances until I saw the first 'Andy Hardy' film one Saturday afternoon, and I was Mickey Rooney again and the embryonic poet disappeared for good.

When the time came for me to sit the Central Welsh Board Examination – the equivalent of GCSEs today, I suppose – I was fairly confident about English, French and Art, but not so happy about Geography and Chemistry, and positively miserable about Maths, Geometry and Algebra. The only theorem I had ever been able to come to terms with was that of Pythagorus – all the rest meant nothing to me.

I have to say that I was in pretty good company, because the form I was in had a reputation for unruly behaviour. Some of the lads had stayed on from the previous year and were sitting the exam a second time. They were consequently that much more advanced in the physical sense, especially one lad, whom I shall refer to only as Dai.

Dai used to come to school on a motorbike – he was just old enough to be allowed to ride one – and sometimes wore plus-fours with his blazer. His moustache was heavier than that of Glan Powell, the form master, and his voice had broken when he was twelve. Naturally, all the class worshipped him.

Nothing bothered Dai, and while the rest of us puffed furtively at fags behind the school toilets, he smoked a pipe quite openly in the yard. The masters had no control over him, but he took no physical liberties with them, regarding them all with an amused cynicism. Everything about him was larger than life – when we had pimples, Dai had boils.

His favourite occupation was perpetrating practical jokes on the masters and sometimes he enrolled our aid. But one day he went too far.

Our maths teacher was an old gentleman with a drooping moustache who loved his pint at lunchtime. On his return from the pub he would set us some arithmetical problem, put his feet on the desk and have a little kip. This was a regular routine, and on the day in question, Dai had decided to have some fun.

He went to a joke shop near the back of the Empire called Dirty Black's, where he bought some stink bombs, sneezing powder and a small, neat pile of imitation dog turds. Armed with these purchases, he returned just before afternoon lessons began and distributed them around the classroom. Somewhat fearfully I took a little pinch of sneezing powder and put it in my waistcoat pocket.

When the maths master came in he followed his customary procedure and settled down, as usual, with his feet on the desk and his mortar-board shielding his pate. After waiting for a snore to emerge from behind the mortar-board, Dai went into action. First he put the pile of dog turds on the open book on the master's desk, and then gave the signal for the other lads to drop the stink bombs. In the excitement I forgot to blow my sneezing powder into the air, but there was enough going on without my adding to the confusion.

The master awoke with a start, removed his mortar-board, saw the mess on his open book and collapsed backwards off his chair. We were all seized with hysteria, banging the desks and yelling in a kind of frenzy – all except Dai, who was observing the scene with quiet satisfaction.

In no time at all the classroom was full of masters and prefects who had heard the noise we were making and were convinced that their worst fears about the Lower Fourth were materializing and that a mutiny had taken place. The sight of them had a sobering effect on our hysteria and very quickly order was restored.

In the recriminations that followed, the Head, Mr 'Beak' John, addressed the form in a quiet voice which was infinitely more frightening than if he had yelled at us.

'Hands up all those boys who had sneezing powder.'

I looked around the class, aware of that little pinch of powder in my waistcoat pocket. Other boys looked down fixedly at the tops of their desks. At home I had always been told to tell the truth whatever the consequences, so slowly I raised my hand, my heart banging away.

'Secombe, eh? And your brother's the head prefect?'

I nodded, unable to speak.

'All right, get outside in the corridor.'

Out of all the boys in the form, only about six of us owned up – Dai, of course, being one of the number.

I was called into the headmaster's study first. I stood before his desk as he eyed me sternly.

'Fred's brother. You've let the family down, and you've let the school down. What have you got to say for yourself?'

'Sorry, sir.' I was determined not to cry. 'I didn't actually use the sneezing powder, sir.' I brought a little bit out of my waistcoat pocket on a finger. The head's nostrils twitched.

'I don't want to cane you, boy. You've never been in trouble before.' His nose twitched again.

I began to breathe more easily.

'Your brother would not want to see you caned, would he?'

I shook my head, convinced now that I'd get off without punishment.

'But if I don't cane you now, you'll only do it again. Hold your hand out.'

He gave me six of the best with his short bamboo cane and I managed not to yell out. As I painfully shut the door behind me I had the meagre satisfaction of hearing a gigantic sneeze.

Dai, who was next in line, grinned widely and winked. 'Good lad,' he said.

Dai ran away from school to join the French Foreign Legion not long after, and his parents had to bring him back. I don't know what became of him in later life, but with his charm and ability to manipulate others he had all the hallmarks of a confidence trickster or a politician. Good luck to you, Dai, wherever you are.

CHAPTER THREE

The Young Tycoon

I left school with a sense of relief mingled with regret that university life was not for me. I had always fancied myself with a scarf in college colours slung carelessly around my neck and an MG ticking away at the kerb, but with my profound ignorance of maths and science I would have been about thirty before I qualified for Higher Certificate. The four credits I had managed to get in English, Art, French and German meant that I had passed the Central Welsh Board Examination, and that would have to suffice.

The time had come to look for a job. The *South Wales Evening Post* 'Positions Vacant' columns became absorbing reading, and I began to apply for interviews. The first one I wrote off for was a vacancy for an insurance clerk in a rather posh firm in Walter Road, Swansea. To my surprise I received a letter in reply asking me to attend the office for an interview. There were quite a few up for the job and from the look of them they were far better qualified than I was. However, I did my best 'Young Woodley' impression and impressed the interviewer enough for him to ask me to come back. Apparently I was on a short list.

The same week I had a letter from Baldwins Ltd, in Wind Street inviting me to go along there in response to my application for the post of junior pay clerk in the Colliery Department. I turned up in my best suit, purchased, as usual,

To whom it may concern.

I have known Harry Donald Secombe 47 Grenfell Park Road, from babyhood. He was one of my Choirboys until his voice broke, and he has always attended Sunday School.

He has been brought up in a good home and has responded well to his training.

He is a well-mannered, well behaved lad, of a quiet and thoughtful disposition, and quite intelligent and dependable.

He has, I believe, the making of a good, useful and valuable man.

He has my best wishes.

E Jenkins Davies
Vicar of St Thomas
Swansea.

Sept: 13th 1937

by my mother with a Provident cheque, one of my father's stiff white collars around my neck and my shoes gleaming from his labours the night before. He set great store by shiny shoes, my Dad.

To cut a long story short, my interview was a success and I was advised to start work the following Monday for the less than princely sum of ten shillings a week. My folks were delighted – some more money coming in and, with luck, a future asured in the commercial world for their somewhat wayward son.

When I arrived for work on the Monday morning I found myself in an office at the end of a long corridor with a glass partition separating it from two other offices – Coal Sales, run by Mr Davies, and Transport, headed by Haydn Baptiste. The lad I was replacing, Ken Thomas, had been promoted to the Post Room, and he was there to initiate me in the role of junior pay clerk. He was a fair-haired, slightly aggressive boy who looked me up and down with an air of disapproval.

'Dynevor boy,' he said, looking at my tie. He was a Glanmor boy himself and there wasn't much love lost between the two schools. 'Here's your most important job,' he said, opening a cupboard. Inside on a stained sheet of brown paper were a cracked jug, half a dozen battered cups, a sugar bowl and a kettle. 'You've got to make tea twice a day – eleven o'clock and four o'clock. You charge 'em a penny a cup.'

So much for the elevated status of junior pay clerk. I was a glorified office boy. Still, I decided to make the most of the situation. I was assigned to Bill Layman, who was responsible for Newlands Colliery pay sheets. He was a kind, bespectacled man who suffered my mistakes with a wry grin. My job – apart from tea making – was to copy out all the details of the colliers' pay from the large pay sheets on to individual dockets. I then had to number each one in sequence with a Roneo machine, a task which made a lot of noise and which I enjoyed. Unfortunately the clatter of my machine made the other members of the office wince.

They were a friendly bunch: Haydn Davies, a burly, pipe-smoking ex-officer, was in charge of Bryn Colliery pay matters; Elvet Thomas, a tall, black-haired young man some three years older than me, was his assistant; Emrys Davies, a wise-cracking man in his early twenties ran Aberbaiden and Mr Brew was in charge of the whole department. Nancy Johns, a tall, pretty blonde who operated the comptometer, was the only female member of the team.

As time went by I became the office clown. I was able to do impressions of some of the staff – an accomplishment which once nearly cost me my job.

It was on a Friday afternoon when, with all the senior members of the department absent at the collieries paying out the miners, Elvet, Nancy and I were alone in the office. The game of firing paper clips from a rubber band at a target on the tea-cupboard door had begun to pall and a desultory silence had descended.

From behind the partition in the Transport Department we heard signs of Haydn Baptiste preparing for an early departure. 'You can hold the fort, Harry,' we could hear him tell his assistant, Harry Vickery.

Elvet tapped me on the arm. 'Go on,' he said. 'Do your J P James impression on the phone.'

J P James was the overall boss of Baldwins' Colliery Office and ruled the place with an iron hand. He also happened to be one of my best impersonations.

I picked up the phone and dialled Haydn's number. He was half-way out of the door when my call rang.

'J P here,' I said.

There were urgent whispers from behind the partition as Harry caught Haydn in mid-flight. 'It's the governor,' he said hoarsely.

'Oh crumbs,' said Hayden, who never swore but often felt like it.

'How many empty wagons have we got at Port Talbot Docks?' I said, J P-like.

'Just a minute, sir.' He turned away and said to Harry, 'Get the figures for Port Talbot Docks.' There followed much searching of ledgers and frantic whispering as the two of them tried to come up with a figure. With empty coal wagons all over the place at Port Talbot Docks, they were faced with a daunting task just when they thought the day was over.

Figures were bandied about which in my role as the boss I pretended to reject. Elvet and Nancy were stuffing handkerchiefs in their mouths to stop themselves giving the game away.

In the end I over-played my hand. 'Bring the ledgers up to my office,' I said, secure in the knowledge that J P James had gone home ages before. When we heard Haydn stagger out of his office loaded with ledgers on his way up three flights of stairs to J P's eyrie at the top of the building, the three of us gave way to hysterics.

What we did not know was that J P James had had a meeting and was still in his office when Haydn tottered in, bearing his pile of ledgers.

'There you are, sir,' he panted, dumping the lot on the boss's desk. 'Count them yourself, sir.'

The governor backed away in alarm as Haydn defended his total of empty wagons. Then the penny dropped.

'It's that new boy – Secombe – he does impressions of you.'

J P James turned to his secretary, Leslie Davies, who told me the story afterwards. 'Get Secombe up here at once,' he said.

I was still laughing downstairs when the furious Head of Transport stormed into our office. 'You're going to cop it,' he said. 'J P wants to see you straight away. That'll teach you.'

My heart was thumping when I reached the glass door of the boss's domain. I knocked with trembling fingers.

'Come in.' J P sat behind his desk with a grim look on his face. He didn't waste time with preliminary chat. 'They tell me you do an impression of me.'

I shuffled, red-faced, before him. 'Er, yes.' There was no point in denying it.

'Let's hear it, then.' He sat back in his chair and folded his arms.

I cleared my throat and attempted to do his bidding. Nothing came out.

'Come along – say "How many empty wagons have we got at Port Talbot Docks?"'

My voice, which could usually break through the sound barrier, refused to function in anything but a broken whisper. 'How – er – many – wagons – have – you – er – got – er – in – Port Talbot Docks?' I croaked, near tears.

J P looked at me for a full half minute, while I saw visions of myself explaining to Mam how I had lost my job.

Finally he spoke. 'Nothing like me at all.' He dismissed me with a wave of his hand.

As I crept thankfully away I heard the sound of laughter.

Having to make tea for everybody still irked me, until one day while waiting for the kettle to boil up in Mrs Puplett's kitchen, I had a brainwave. Mrs Puplett was the wife of the commissionaire and was responsible for the catering. She had to provide teas and light lunches for the bosses of the Steel Department as well as for J P James himself, and had a couple of huge teapots always on the go.

'Any chance of buying one of those teapots?' I asked her. 'If I had one like that I could extend my tea round and make it pay off.'

She was a good old soul, and had travelled the world as the wife of Sergeant-Major Alf Puplett who, with waxed moustache and immaculate uniform, kept unwanted visitors at bay at the front door of the Head Office building. For some reason she had taken quite a liking to me.

'Tell you what,' she said. 'I'll get you a new one and you can pay me when you can.'

I was delighted and began to make plans for my venture into tea-making on the grand scale. No more broken cups and chipped saucers for me. I went to the china stall in

Swansea Market and bought a dozen cheap but whole cups and saucers. Next, I had a chat with Mr Goldsworthy, the grocer whose shop was opposite the front of the office, and negotiated a good price for not too broken biscuits. A new tin tray completed my tea set, and I was ready for business.

The size of the teapot meant that I was able to take a lot more customers on, and with the broken biscuits in each saucer as a 'come on', I was able to up the price of a cup of tea to three ha'pence. Before long I had spread my tentacles all over the office building. Eventually I was earning more money from tea-making than from clerking and was becoming known as Joe Lyons Junior.

Looking back on those days from this distance in time my recollections are to say the least kaleidoscopic. I remember being happy with my lot: I had a ready-made audience in most of my work-mates, though some found my boisterous nature a bit hard to take. Odd memories do stand out though, with a quite startling clarity.

One day I shall never forget was when Bill Layman returned to the office after an operation for gall stones. We all gave him a great welcome back because he really was a very popular fellow. He had brought with him in a matchbox lined with cotton wool the stones which had been giving him so much trouble. They looked remarkably like the sweets we used to have in those days called marzipan bon-bons, being brown and crystalline in appearance. Bill was quite proud of his trophies and passed them around for us all to admire.

One person who had not joined the group which had collected to greet our returned invalid was an old gentleman who worked in the Coal Sales. His name was Joe Meagher and he was a special mate of mine. He was in his sixties and was profoundly deaf, the result of a boating accident in the Bristol Channel. If anyone wanted to tell him something, he always had a pad and pencil on his desk so that the message could be written down.

This particular morning he was completely absorbed in his work and was not aware of what was going on in the pay department. I was determined to bring him up to date with all the excitement and, with Bill Layman's somewhat reluctant permission, I borrowed one of his gall stones to show to Joe in the other room. I tapped him on the shoulder and held out my left hand containing the gall stone, then reached for the pad with my right hand to write down what it was.

Joe looked up, saw the shiny object in my hand and popped it into his mouth, thinking it to be a sweet. I stared at him aghast as he thanked me and bent his head back to his writing, crunching away as he did.

Frantically I wrote 'Bill Layman's gall stone' and pushed the pad under his nose. He read it, still chomping, then with a strangled cry headed for the toilet at the end of the corridor.

Bill Layman was not very happy at losing one of his treasures, and poor old Joe went home. A memorable day indeed.

Another vivid memory remains of the day I was taken from the office to my mother's hospital bedside. She had been admitted for an operation for kidney stones after months of terrible back pains. It was shortly after Bill Layman's own operation, and he had been most kind to me when he knew that Mam had been taken to hospital, allaying my fears and playing down the seriousness of the situation. However, when the call came from the hospital requesting me to attend, I was in a terrible state. My brother was in college and my father was off on his rounds of the grocers' shops and could not be contacted.

Apparently the surgeon had opened her up – awful phrase – and discovered that the kidney was useless and had to be removed. She was in such a bad way that they decided to send for the next-of-kin straight away.

The next couple of hours were a nightmare. I sat holding my mother's hand, willing her to live and trying not to cry; a boy sent to do a man's job. I couldn't imagine what life would be like without her. Mam was the strong one of the family –

the dynamo who kept everything ticking over, who treated all three children alike, but made each of us feel special.

For a long while there was no response from the hand I held so tightly. Then I felt a gentle squeeze and she opened her eyes and smiled, and I could have run up Kilvey Hill a dozen times for her. I made a mental vow never to give her any cause to worry about me ever again. But I did, I'm afraid. I joined the Territorial Army.

In April 1939, Hore-Belisha, the War Minister at the time, introduced conscription. When war broke out on 3 September, anyone over the age of 18 and up to 41 years old was, subject to passing the medical examination, liable to be called up to serve eighteen months in the services. The only way to escape the conscription net was by joining the Territorials. This meant reporting once a week to the barracks and spending two weeks away in camp.

There were several men in the Head Office who were eligible for call-up. Johnny Otterson, who was the assistant to Leslie Davies, and Emrys Davies of the Pay Department were two of them. They decided to opt for the Territorials and consequently joined the 132nd Field Regiment Royal Artillery (TA), with the result that they would both be away at the same time for summer camp. And as I helped out Johnny Otterson in the Post Room some of his work would fall on me.

I thought carefully about this, and decided I would follow their example. The only snag being that I was not yet eighteen. However, Johnny told me that nobody asked for a birth certificate and that it was easy to get in.

Another thing which swayed me was the fact that war was definitely going to come sooner or later. My father had been an infantry soldier and I had heard enough stories about his First World War experiences not to want to follow his example. The Royal Artillery, though, seemed a much better proposition. It required clerks and specialists, and to be perfectly honest I fancied myself in breeches and spurs, which was the uniform of an artilleryman at that time.

Mam went very quiet when I told her that I was joining my mates, but she accepted the fact with a sigh. My father was secretly pleased that I was going to be a 'five-mile sniper' as he called it.

The only trouble I envisaged was passing the eye test at my medical. My eyesight, without spectacles, was still extremely poor, but I could see perfectly well with them on. When the time came for me to see the doctor at the Drill Hall, I had already learned the eye chart from memory, thanks to Johnny Otterson. He had copied it out for me beforehand. Thus, when I had stripped off, blushed and allowed my head to be searched for nits, I rattled off all the letters on the chart down to the printer's name.

'Remarkable,' said the MO with a twinkle in his eye. 'All right, son, if you're that keen to join the Terriers, you're in.'

I was given an army number, a second-hand uniform and the rank of Gunner. Hitler in his eyrie at Berchtesgarten must have felt just a slight *frisson* of foreboding. I'm sure Neville Chamberlain did.

'Sex appeal in brackets,' was my family's unanimous decision when they first saw me in my puttees and spurs, looking bandy-legged in the somewhat clown-like breeches, and with a tunic that had taken on a greenish tinge with age. But I fancied myself in the uniform, trying all sorts of military poses in the big mirror in my parents' bedroom. 'Not bad,' I thought to myself, turning smartly. I caught one spur in the other and crashed to the floor.

The regiment went to camp in July and we all began to feel what real soldiering was all about. We were under canvas on Malvern Links in Worcestershire for two weeks, and the sergeants really put us through it. The officers were as raw as we were, with one or two exceptions, and mostly concerned with being saluted. After two weeks a lot of friendships had been cemented and a few enemies made, but it was all smiles when we broke camp. We tossed our Sergeant-Major in the air in a blanket, nearly breaking his neck in the process; not realizing that in a few short weeks we were to be soldiers in earnest and that Sergeant-Majors have long memories.

War had been in the air for some time and it clouded everything we did that summer. But it still came as a shock.

I have particular reason to remember the day I was called up. It was a Friday and I was at Newlands Colliery with Bill Layman that morning preparing to pay out. Briefly, what happened on these occasions was that, along with the Chief Clerk at the Colliery, we would put the money for each miner in a tin with a number on it. The number would correspond with that on a counterfoil called a pay docket. Each docket would show what each miner was entitled to, and was made up by the clerks at Head Office from the pay sheets which were sent down to us from the Colliery. The person responsible for numbering each docket with its tear-off counterfoil was myself. I used a Roneo machine which stamped the numbers twice on each docket, and when I had finished I was supposed to check each ticket with the pay sheets to make sure that all numbers were correct. The pay dockets were then sent back to Newlands by rail so that the tins could be prepared. All that happened at the Colliery then was that the miner would hand in his numbered counterfoil and he'd receive the money from the tin with the corresponding number on it.

However, owing to the heavy amount of business I was doing on my tea round – I had even extended to an office across the road which had nothing to do with Baldwins – I did the tickets in a hurry. It was getting near to the train time and so instead of checking each ticket individually from the pay sheets, I just made sure that the first and last numbers tallied. What I was not aware of was that the Roneo machine, owing no doubt to its enthusiastic handling, had slipped and in consequence some of the numbers were out of order. However it had righted itself some twenty tickets later and the last digits were correct.

The first few miners were soon dealt with as they handed in their slips through the pigeon-hole in our corrugated iron pay office and I happily handed down the tins from the shelves around the walls. Then, slowly, a trickle of men began to bang on the side of the office demanding attention.

'I done five shifts at 7/6d and I've only got half a crown.'

'What's going on in there? My butty's got the wrong money . . .' etc. etc.

The shouting got louder and the banging more insistent and Arthur Kingdom, the Chief Clerk of Newlands, slammed the door shut over the pigeon-hole. He and Bill Layman turned to me.

'Did you check the tickets, Secombe?' It had been 'Harry' all morning.

'Sorry,' I said weakly.

Outside the miners were getting angrier as they counted their money, and the clamour reached frightening proportions as we tried to put things right.

Suddenly there came the cry of someone in authority. 'Come out, Secombe.'

I backed away in a corner. I thought I might be lynched – I'd seen too many Westerns to think otherwise. But it was not a lynch mob, it was the Seventh Cavalry in the shape of Adolf Hitler.

'You've been called up, son.'

'Thank God,' I said.

CHAPTER FOUR

Playing Soldiers

We lined up among the tents, the uneasy laughter hushed, and listened to Neville Chamberlain on the radio making his reluctant declaration of war. One thing is for sure, I thought, we're not playing at soldiers any more.

It was Sunday, 3 September and we had been detailed to strike the tents which had housed other Territorials from a Nottinghamshire regiment who had been camping at Parkmill on the Gower coast.

Only a few weeks earlier my family had rented a bungalow in a field not far away in Pennard and, where we now stood, a travelling fair had blared out 'South Of The Border' and 'Roll Out The Barrel'. Our task was to pack up all the gear the other lads had left behind and load it on to lorries which would take it back to the Midlands.

There was an air of unreality about everything we did in those first few weeks of the phoney war. There didn't seem to be any kind of order and at the very beginning we were even allowed to stay at home. This was a bit embarrassing for me, because after I had reported to the Drill Hall on the Friday evening I was sent home and told to report the following morning. Consequently on Saturday morning I made a big farewell tour of the patch and St Leger Crescent as I was driven to war. Archie Roberts, a friend of Fred's and mine, possessed a Daimler car of which we were all extremely envious. The only means of private transport available to most of the denizens of Grenfell Park Estate were push–bikes. The sight of a car in our street usually brought out a posse of kids to sit on its running boards to have their photographs taken. So when Archie offered to drive me back to the Drill Hall, I made the most of it.

The car had a sunshine roof, and by standing on the front passenger seat I was able to emerge in true VIP style to wave to the neighbours, who stood at their front gates to see me off. With the aid of a black pocket comb I performed my locally celebrated impression of Adolf Hitler to the accompaniment of good-natured boos from the onlookers. The only person who seemed apprehensive was Archie, who winced as he saw the damage my army boots were doing to his front seat.

Of course, I was sent back home again that afternoon, and although I had to report for duty at Parkmill on the Sunday, I made so many farewell appearances that I became a bit of a joke. Men who had waved goodbye to me from their gates were in the British Expeditionary Force in France while I was still hanging about the district.

For a while we were billeted in a dance hall in Neath, just a few miles outside Swansea, and then we went to Carmarthen for three weeks where we were stationed in Lamas Street Barracks. The food there was dreadful, and at night most of us haunted the local fish and chip shops rather than tackle what our sergeant cook had to offer us. We had to queue up with our mess-tins at lunch-time and the contents of an old Soyer stove were slopped into them. The official title was 'stew', but the concoction contained ingredients which were too awful to contemplate, and there was strong evidence that an old army boot provided the basis for the stock. However, anyone with the temerity to complain had to face the fury of the sergeant cook, who was ready to rush out from his kitchen with a butcher's knife at the slightest sign of criticism. Fortunately for us all he was discharged from the regiment for being mentally unstable, and by the time we had settled in at our next destination – Usk – the standard of cuisine had risen slightly.

The place itself was very forbidding – as well it might be, because it was a recently vacated Borstal Institution, which before that had been an adult prison. Inside the high walls and behind the big green door it was just like a scene from one of the 'Big House' epics which Hollywood turned out so often in the Thirties. The two-tiered rows of cells radiated like the spokes of a wheel from the hub of the central hallway. Wire mesh was stretched across the cell wings separating the top row from the bottom one, and trestle tables and wooden forms were placed in the space between the cells. We were allocated two to a cell and were given straw palliasses upon which to sleep. This was to be our home for the next six months or so, and this was where we were going to be made into proper soldiers, whether we liked it or not.

Up until November, the regiment consisted of two gun batteries – 321, the Swansea Territorials, and 322 battery, the Neath volunteers – and the strength numerically was only about 250 men. We had started the war with eight 4.5 gun howitzers which were taken from us to go to Finland. They were replaced by iron-tyred guns. The transport which drew these guns and carried us to and fro around the area consisted of a varied assortment of pop lorries, brewer's drays and officers' cars. The two Scammells which pulled 322 Battery's guns were bright scarlet in colour and could not be painted dark because they were on hire for a pound a day.

I belonged at this time to the specialist section, as did most of the lads I joined up with. We were all clerks of some kind and regarded as potential NCOs or possibly officer material. We formed the basis for the office staff of both batteries and were being trained in the mysteries of how to direct the fire of the guns, an art I was never fully to master because it involved complicated mathematics.

My particular friend then was Danny Williams, an athletic lad about two years older than me. We used to sit up at nights at the tables between the cells discussing philosophy, the quality of the beer in the pubs, and the possible availability of the barmaids. Another mate was D K Griffiths, a jolly type with a moustache that made him look older than his years. Everybody wanted him as a friend because of his ability to play the piano. When he sat down at a pub piano to do his celebrated Charlie Kunz impressions the drinks were always on the house for D K and his mates in uniform. Sometimes I'd join in after a pint or two and do some of my bits and pieces, which usually resulted in a packet of crisps being hurled my way. I still had a long way to go as a performer.

The winter of '39 was a particularly severe one and the snow piled up everywhere. The heating in the cell blocks was not very effective and soon a lot of the boys were coming down with all sorts of ailments. There were a few cases of scarlet fever, some caught pneumonia, and the first flush of excitement had evaporated in the dreary drilling and training. I remember one incident that gave us all a laugh one weekend, although it backfired in the end.

One of the specialists among us was Gunner Thomas A C G, known to one and all, for some unaccountable reason, as 'Titty–bottle' Thomas. I had known him before the war when he worked in an office on the Swansea docks. He was always a good source for postage stamps at a cut price.

At the end of our row of cells was the padded cell in which those prisoners who were getting a bit too stroppy had been incarcerated until they cooled off. It was too dilapidated for use as living quarters, so it was left locked – that is, until one Saturday afternoon when one of the lads with nothing to do managed to open the lock with a screw driver. Then someone had the bright idea of getting old 'Titty-bottle' to enter the cell and shutting him in there for a lark.

I can't remember what ruse we employed to get him to go in – it must have been a dare of some kind. Anyway, in he went and we slammed the door on him, intending to let him out after a few minutes. He pounded away on the mildewed padding for a while, shouting and yelling at us, and then Danny Williams, who had a natural authority even though he had no rank, said, 'All right, that's enough, let the lad out.' Unfortunately, the lock had sprung and no amount of sweating and straining could shift the cell door – after all, those doors were supposed to stay shut. Poor old Thomas was getting hysterical by this time, and the RSM was summoned. He read the situation at a glance, and turning on the half a dozen or so of us who were gathered around the cell door he said, 'There's no chance of getting a locksmith up from Newport at the weekend. He's got to stay there till Monday, and you clever buggers are going to sit here outside this door and keep him company.'

And that's what we had to do. We managed to open the iron flap in the door through which food was passed in the old days, and kept up a non-stop conversation with poor 'Titty-bottle', taking it in turns to read to him and pass him the odd bottle of beer. Most of us had made arrangements to do other things that weekend, but the RSM made us keep up our vigil until the locksmith arrived from Newport early on Monday morning and released a tearful Thomas. It didn't appear to have done him much harm, because he left us for an officer training course not long after, and finished the war as a Lieutenant-Colonel in the Intelligence Corps. I finished up as a Lance-Bombardier – and I was on the outside.

We stayed in the prison up to the time of Dunkirk, when some of us were detailed to meet the ships coming in to Newport docks from the beaches. Our job was to help the chaps ashore and take them back to Usk to clean them up and provide them with fresh kit.

I'll never forget seeing those soldiers – real soldiers, not like us – bandaged and unshaven, and for the most part grim and unsmiling, their eyes full of what they had just gone through. I felt ashamed and ineffectual as we directed them to the waiting trucks and, for the first time since the war started, I realized what my uniform was all about.

There was one unbearably poignant incident that day. A soldier who had escaped completely unscathed from France, and had just been kitted out with a fresh uniform, crossed the road from the prison to send a telegram home to tell his family that he was safe and well. On the way back, a few minutes later, he was knocked down by a lorry and killed. That took some getting over for all of us.

With the war having taken a more dramatic turn, training was intensified and the regiment was strengthened by reservists and militiamen. After several local moves, we found ourselves deployed along the South Wales coast with no infantry and eight guns. We had to look after about sixty miles of coast and our ammunition consisted of one hundred very old rounds per gun. (I quote from the regimental history, so I'm not making it up.)

One day we were taken down to the seaside near Margam to watch one of the guns being fired. Our officers thought it would be a good idea for us to see just what a howitzer could do. The gun was manhandled down on to the shore and we were all instructed to get well behind it and watch. The gun was loaded with due ceremony and the order was given to fire. There was a flash, the shell landed with a disconcertingly light plop about two hundred yards out to sea, and a wheel fell off the gun carriage. Of course, we all fell about with laughter.

As specialists we were detailed to take turns with our officers at an observation post which had been set up on the dunes at Margam, and one morning it was my turn to take over just before dawn after a heavy air raid on Port Talbot. I was equipped with a revolver which I had never fired and an officer named Major Sims, who always seemed to regard me with a kind of detached amusement. A few weeks before this incident he had passed me out as a driver, on the strict condition that I was never to drive a lorry within three miles of where he happened to be. I had demolished three concrete posts in Usk cattle market during the course of my test. 'I like your style, Secombe,' he said, signing my licence application with a flourish.

We arrived together at the dug-out in the dunes and my head was still buzzing with the events of the night before. It had been a nasty raid on Port Talbot and we were told to be on the look out for parachutists. This was the period when we were expecting an invasion at any time – well, I certainly was.

After we'd been at the observation post for about half an hour, Major Sims decided he had to go back to HQ for some reason, leaving me in complete possession of the fire power. It was still fairly dark when he left and I squinted fearfully into the expanse of sand before me. Off to the right I could just about make out some smoke from the direction of Port Talbot and as my eyes came back from looking at it I thought I saw movement in the near foreground. Sweatily I reached for the binoculars and trained them on what I thought I'd seen. Sure enough there was something there. My glasses steamed up with fear and I had difficulty focusing the heavy army binoculars. It was definitely a man in uniform of some sort, and he had a bicycle with him. We'd been warned about parachutists with bicycles.

I was transfixed with terror as the figure crept nearer, then I forced my trembling fingers to ease the big 45 from its holster. It was getting lighter, but not enough to distinguish what kind of uniform the figure before me was wearing. 'Who goes there?' I yodelled. No reply. I said it again, and pointed the wobbling weapon in the figure's general direction. I knew it was loaded but I was not sure where the safety-catch was. Trembling like a leaf I fumbled around trying to find it. 'Oh God, oh Mam,' I was saying mindlessly over and over. 'Halt or I fire,' I croaked for the last time, and shut my eyes, taking a fearful first pressure on the trigger.

'Hello there,' said a cheerful Welsh voice. 'Playing soldiers here, are you?' A postman stood before the entrance to the dug-out. 'Thought I'd look in on the way to work. I was in the Welch Fusiliers in the last lot, cosmopolitan crowd we were.' He seemed prepared for a long chat. 'Be careful with that thing,' he said, pointing to the revolver in my hand. 'You can kill somebody, mun.' He was quite surprised when I began to cry.

We moved from Usk to a country mansion at a place called Clytha, not far from Abergavenny, where we were put under canvas, a great relief to all after the shocking conditions we had suffered in the prison. It was a time of route marches through the lovely Monmouthshire countryside, and often the wild life would be disturbed by the harsh tones of Adolf Hitler as I led the column doing my by now celebrated impression with the pocket comb. I was pretty firmly established as the regimental idiot, a role I found to be rather useful on one or two occasions.

I was on leave one weekend from Clytha, and while walking down Swansea High Street with my pal from the regiment, 'Dixie' Deans, I was arrested by an over-zealous Redcap for being improperly dressed. To compound the felony I had left my AB64 – my army pay book and identification document at home along with my weekend pass. The result was that I was put under arrest in the Military Police HQ in Swansea High Street railway station until Dixie got back with my means of identification. Dixie said that when he told my mother what had happened she burst out laughing. I was released and told that I would be reported to my regiment and consequently, on my return from leave, I was called up before the Battery Commander, Major Thomas.

I was marched in along with Dixie as a witness and the charges against me were duly read out by the Sergeant-Major. 'Improperly dressed, not in possession of his AB64 and leave pass, and insisting on whistling the German national anthem when in custody.'

Major Thomas's mouth twitched under his large brown moustache. 'Is that the lot?' he said.

'Yessir,' said the Sergeant-Major.

The major looked down at his desk for a moment and then looked up. 'Sergeant-Major, as you well know, Gunner Secombe is not responsible for his actions. Case dismissed.'

Major Thomas featured in another episode, this time one in which my reputation played against me. I had applied for an officers' training course after seeing a notice in regimental orders referring to an urgent need for officers in the Indian Army. I seemed to have all the necessary scholastic qualifications – the Establishment was obviously getting desperate – and so I filled in an application form. A week or two later I was on fatigue duty, unloading coal from a lorry, when I was summoned to the battery office. 'No time to change,' said the messenger. 'Go as you are.'

I duly found myself standing to attention in a pair of filthy overalls, my face smudged and my glasses askew.

Major Thomas sat at his desk with my application form before him. He was obviously under some stress. Across the office, Bombardier Otterson was also suffering from a deep emotional crisis.

'Ah, Secombe,' began my battery commander, his fingers fiddling with his moustache. 'I see you've applied for a commission. . .' He broke off and held his head in his hands for a moment. Then he looked up at me and could no longer contain himself. He began to laugh, silently at first, then he started to cackle. Otterson, my erstwhile comrade from Baldwins, was pounding his desk as an accompaniment to his wild whooping laughter.

I still stood at attention, my dreams of gin slings and punkah wallahs and a starched khaki drill uniform with a gleaming Sam Browne dissipating rapidly. I was hurt – cut to the quick. And then I caught sight of my reflection in the window behind the major's desk. God! Was that me? The merriment was infectious and for several minutes we clung together, the three of us fused with laughter, until eventually I stumbled out of the battery office clutching my aching stomach. And that was as near as I ever got to becoming an officer. Some of my friends did go as officers to the Far East and were taken prisoner almost as soon as they got off the boat. There's a lesson in there somewhere.

My nineteenth birthday found me in Staffordshire at a place called Rugely. The town had one claim to fame – Dr Palmer, a notorious poisoner, had lived there, and it was the favourite joke in the battery that he was still around and working in the cookhouse. It was 8 September 1940, and the day that our fighter aircraft brought down a record number of enemy planes. That night I was on guard duty in a bell-tent at the entrance to the camp alongside an ornamental lake.

Ammunition was so short that there was only one magazine for all four sentries, and as each one came off duty he had to unload it from his own rifle and hand it over to the next man on sentry-go. At this time our 303 rifles had been taken from us for more deserving soldiers and we were issued with ancient Canadian Ross rifles which, unlike the Lee-Enfields we were used to, had no cut-out. The cut-out was a piece of metal which, when depressed, prevented the bullet from being loaded into the breech. To operate this cut-out, you pulled back the bolt, pushed the metal plate over the contents of the magazine and then slid the bolt back home over the empty breech and pulled the trigger. As I said, the Ross rifles did not have this safety precaution.

It was warm that night and some of the sentries were sleeping outside the tent on groundsheets because it was cooler by the lakeside. However, because I found the gnats a nuisance, I had opted to sleep inside the tent. When my turn came to take up my post, I sleepily loaded the magazine that had been tossed to me by the man I was relieving, pulled back the bolt, operated an imaginary cut-out, pointed the rifle to-wards the wall of the tent and, after pushing home the bolt, pressed the trigger. There was one hell of a bang, and a hole appeared in the tent wall. There was a loud yell, followed by splashing sounds, and then another shout, more high-pitched this time.

What had happened was like a scene from a Laurel and Hardy comedy. The bullet had penetrated the ground near where Gunner Haydn was sleeping. He woke up with a start and instinctively ran into the lake, where he stubbed his bare toes on a wooden crate of Molotov cocktails which had been put in the water to keep them stable. His yells and the rifle shot brought the duty officer running down the path in his pyjama top, revolver at the ready. 'Call out the mobile,' he cried, invoking what was supposed to be a flying column of guns which was to go into action immediately the invasion began. (When they were called out a couple of days later on a false alarm only the gun towed by a pop lorry made it to the rendezvous – all the others broke down.)

Then he saw me at the entrance to the tent, still in a state of shock, with a smoking rifle in my hands. 'Oh shit,' he said. He turned back to the other men, who were now running down the path behind him to find out what the fuss was all about. 'It's all right, it's only Secombe.'

This time I did go on a charge – for wasting ammunition. I got off with a few days confined to barracks which, under the circumstances, was pretty lenient.

By Christmas 1940 the regiment had undergone a period of intensive training in Aldershot and 496 Battery was formed from personnel from my Battery, the 321, our sister Battery, 322, and a fresh intake from London. From being a wholly Welsh regiment at the start of the war, we now became a mixture of cockneys and northerners – and for the first time I heard myself being called 'Taffy'.

In spite of myself I was gradually becoming more proficient as a soldier – not enough to keep Hitler awake at night, but I now knew how to fire a rifle properly, and the workings of the 75mm guns which we had been issued in September were no longer a completely closed book. One thing I wasn't too bad at was the drawing of a panorama, which was a sketch of the countryside viewed from an observation post. I liked drawing little trees and smoke coming out of the chimneys of the farmhouses and cottages which were our imaginary targets. When I began to put in cows and horses my officer, Captain Gordon Davies, would remonstrate with me. 'Come on, Secombe. You're a gunner not a Constable.' There was no answer to that, although it was around this time what I was working on the 'raspberry' or the Bronx cheer which was to become a feature of my variety act a few years thence.

I spent most of my time working in the battery office along with Johnny Otterson, who was the chief clerk, and Ken Jenkins, with whom I was responsible for making out the acquittance rolls, or pay sheets, for the battery pay parade. There seemed to be no escape from adding up figures, although there was no chance of a repeat of my Baldwins fiasco. Ken Jenkins supervised my figures and he was a phenomenal mathematician. He also knew the name, rank and number of every member of the battery. By nature he was a nice, quiet, kind sort of bloke and I'm afraid my boisterous nature must have got on his nerves at times, though he never showed it. On the other hand, Bombardier Otterson was not averse to heaving an ebony ruler in my direction.

Danny Williams was now a bombardier with two sparkling stripes on his arm, and one day he came to me and said, 'How would you fancy a trip to Scotland with me?'

It appeared that he had been detailed to collect a prisoner from Maryhill Barracks, Glasgow. The man – whose name, incidentally, was Jack Dempsey – had not returned from leave and had been arrested as a deserter. He hadn't been with the battery very long and neither of us knew him by sight. 'It's a nice little trip, Harry,' said Dan, and I accepted readily. We drew our rail passes and haversack rations and headed for the station.

The journey up to Glasgow was not very comfortable and we were forced to sit most of the way in the corridor. 'Don't worry,' said Dan. 'On the way back I've got authority to commandeer a reserved compartment because we'll be bringing back a prisoner.'

'That'll be nice, Dan,' I said, stepping on my haversack rations as I stood up to let an officer go past.

Danny's intention was to report to Maryhill Barracks that evening, spend the night in the YMCA, and pick up the prisoner in the morning. However, the moment we stepped through the entrance of the barracks in Sauchiehall Street we were made to double march across the parade ground by an aggressive sergeant-major. In the guard room we were stood to attention while the prisoner was brought in from the cells.

'Gunner Dempsey,' said a laconic sergeant, handing over a short, nervous lad wearing spotless battledress. Danny signed for him and then the three of us were marched back across the parade ground and out into the street.

'Sorry to cause you all this trouble,' said our prisoner.

'Don't mention it,' I said cheerfully.

Danny gave me a hard look. After all, he was in charge.

It transpired that poor old Dempsey had gone home on compassionate leave because his home had been bombed in an air raid and he couldn't get everything sorted out in the forty-eight hours he had been given. We felt sorry for the lad, and when we had settled down in the compartment Danny had duly commandeered, we treated him to a bottle of beer from the station buffet.

By the time we arrived in London we were fast friends, and after breakfast at a Church Army mobile canteen, Danny decided that, as we had plenty of time to spare before getting the train back to Aldershot, we'd take a little walk around the Victoria area. We went to a cartoon cinema, had a few beers in a pub, and then Danny looked at his watch and declared that we'd better get cracking. Before catching the train we were supposed to report to the RTO at Victoria Station, which involved us getting into a lift. By this time Dempsey was carrying my rifle over his shoulder, because my shoulder was getting sore. There was the usual crush of servicemen in the station, laden like us with equipment, and as the lift arrived there was a surge forward and Dempsey was thrust into the lift in front of us. The gates shut and we watched open-mouthed as our charge disappeared upwards without us. Danny and I looked at each other in alarm and then started for the stairs, only to be impeded by a solid phalanx of Canadian servicemen coming down them. By the time we reached the top of the stairs the lift had gone down again and there was no sign of Dempsey. We ran back down, having to push our way through the soldiers, only to find the lift on its way back up, and still no glimpse of our prisoner.

We sat down on a bench and discussed the situation calmly. 'He's gone – he's deserted again. Oh God, oh Mam, what are we going to do? He's got my rifle. It's the glasshouse for me.'

'Shut up,' said Danny. 'We'll have to tell the RTO we've lost our prisoner, that's all we can bloody well do.'

I had wild thoughts of pretending to lose my memory and wandering off into the crowds. I had played a blind beggar in John Masefield's *Good Friday* with the St Thomas Players and had perfected a marvellous out-of-focus look. It would come in handy now. Danny took a firm grip on the back of my battledress jacket and propelled me towards the lift again. As we turned the corner, there on a bench outside the RTO's office was Gunner Dempsey, looking very anxious. 'Where've you been? I've just reported that I've lost my escort.' We grabbed him thankfully and hustled him away.

I'm glad to say that he was dealt with very mercifully by the commanding officer, and after a week's detention he was allowed to go back home on leave to attend to his family.

By the time spring came in 1941 the regiment was posted down to Sussex in an anti-invasion role. It was a pleasant part of the world to be stationed, and our battery's temporary home was Gote Farm near Ditchling, just below the wooded 'V' on the northern slopes of the South Downs. The battery office was set up in the farmhouse itself, with the Battery Commander and some of his officers billeted in the bedrooms on the first floor. Behind the main farmhouse the barn had become the officers' mess. The BC was new to us and obviously on his way to a higher command in the future. His name was Major Townend, his manner brusque but fair. He had a clipped, no-nonsense way of talking which I found fascinating. It was the way officers spoke in films – most of our lot from the TA days had more than a leavening of Welsh in their speech. This man was a pukka sahib and I managed to work up a pretty good impression of him. It was soon to get me into trouble once again.

During this period in Sussex, the officers were going through very intensive training. It was a far cry from the very early days of the war when some of the specialists had to carry their officers through the trickiest methods of bringing down fire on the enemy. There was one lieutenant who was sent on quite an extensive course on hygiene in the field. When he returned he was detailed to give his first lecture to the specialists and signallers. He assembled us and addressed us thus: 'If there's one thing I've learned, it's this. Don't kick the turd about – bury it. Now, who's got a pack of cards?' And that was it. We were very sorry to lose him.

Things had changed, and there were tactical exercises without the presence of the lower orders called TEWT (Tactical Exercises Without Troops), of which Major Townend was particularly fond.

One morning he set off early on one of these TEWTs, leaving me in complete control of the battery office. Only Townend's batman, Protheroe, was left behind. His job was to light the fire in the office grate and tidy up generally while I got on with the laborious job of typing out the battery correspondence with one finger.

Protheroe was not exactly a ball of fire, and given the opportunity was not averse to using his officer's camp bed to kip on when the latter was out. He was a grizzled soldier with an armful of long-service stripes. At eight o'clock on what had started off a lovely sunny day, but which was now beginning to cloud over, Protheroe had still not made an appearance. No amount of persuasion would induce him to come down and take over his duties. I resorted to a desperate measure. Tiptoeing out through the front door I made a great fuss of entering and slamming the door behind me. Then, using my Townend voice, I called up the stairs from the hallway.

'Protheroe,' I yelled. 'Come down here.'

There was a muffled cry from the major's bedroom and a dishevelled batman appeared at the top of the stairs, hastily buttoning his trousers. When he saw it was me and not the Battery Commander he let fly with a few choice phrases picked up in various parts of the empire, including some in Urdu. He then went back into Townend's bedroom and banged the door shut.

There wasn't much I could do about making him come down to carry out his chores – I was only a gunner like him – so I muttered a few oaths of my own and lit the fire myself. Afterwards I went back to my painful typing.

Outside the sky darkened and a light rain began, which gradually became heavier. Then, in the distance, came the sound of a motor bike putt-putting down the path to the farmhouse. It was, of course, the Battery Commander, who had gone off earlier without his mackintosh. He was now on his way back to collect it.

From my typewriter, as if in a dream, I watched open-mouthed as Major Townend stepped damply over the threshold and slammed the front door shut behind him. He shook the rain off his cap, gave me a curt nod and went to the foot of the stairs.

'Protheroe,' he shouted.

'Eff off,' cried his batman, who was lying on his back on the camp bed smoking one of the BC's Perfectos cigarettes, his uniform shed and strewn on the floor.

Major Townend turned to me in complete disbelief. I raised my eyebrows in a travesty of surprise.

Once again he called, this time adding Protheroe's rank. A fresh outburst of abuse came from upstairs, including a few sexual suggestions which I found quite remarkable.

The major took the stairs three at a time and, strangely calm and aware of the outcome, I followed him. As Townend opened the bedroom door I was able to get the full reaction on Protheroe's face as he stood to attention in his long johns, his wedding tackle swinging in the breeze. Smoke rose from the cigarette cupped in one hand, and a whimper came from his open mouth. Then he saw me and said, as Haydn Baptiste had said only a couple of years before, 'I thought it was Secombe, sir. He takes you off.'

Townend fixed me with a steely eye. 'Does he, by God?'

I shrugged my shoulders helplessly.

'I'll deal with you later,' he said to me and turned back to his by now ex-batman. 'Get out at once and report to the Battery Sergeant-Major.' He grabbed his mac from behind the door and marched angrily down the stairs.

I was still typing away late into the evening, wondering fearfully what my fate would be, when I heard a roar of laughter from the officers' mess in the barn behind the farmhouse. Shortly after, the BC came into the office with a glass of brandy in his hand. He put it down on the army blanket covering the trestle table which served as my desk.

'Drink this,' he said. 'I've been with this regiment for some weeks now, and that was the first laugh I've had from my officers. I told them about Protheroe.' He barked a short laugh and left, smiling.

Later he was to become a headmaster famous for his unorthodox methods. I thought he was a great chap, but I never did an impression of him again – I felt it would have been extremely dangerous.

Ditchling was, and is, a pretty little town and its inhabitants didn't seem to mind too much that their pubs and institutions were being taken over by the army. I managed to get involved with the local concert party which was run by an extremely nice girl called Joy, who was a school teacher. She persuaded me to agree to perform in a variety concert at the Town Hall.

I made a list of my impressions – Stainless Stephen, a Sheffield comedian who always announced that he was speaking from the 'B full stop B ditto C ditto Studios, London full stop; then there was Sandy Powell – 'Can you hear me, mother?'; Stanley Holloway reciting 'Albert and the Lion', and Windy, the toothless sidekick of Hopalong Cassidy, the cowboy star. Not exactly show-stopping material, but I was learning to handle an audience. I would usually finish with a falsetto rendering of a Deanna Durbin song which always seemed to go down well. However, I was always careful to blow a few raspberries in the middle of it, just in case anyone got the wrong idea.

Everything was going well on the night of the concert, until someone introduced me to a pint of old and mild followed by a whisky chaser. I thought it was a great innovation, especially as I was being treated, and my confidence increased as I tried it again. Across from the pub the concert was proceeding apace with the local talent scoring heavily with the mixed audience of servicemen and civilians. I was the life and soul of the pub, and when my time came to go back to the concert I strode confidently towards the stage door. Unfortunately the mixture I had been drinking hit me as I got half-way, and by the time I arrived backstage my legs could hardly support me.

Joy eyed me anxiously as I assured her with nods and winks that I was fine and ready to paralyse the audience. Reluctantly she informed the compère that I was all set for my entrance and I stepped sweatily on to the stage.

What happened after that I cannot remember very clearly. I know that I got all the impressions mixed up and my Deanna Durbin song was punctuated with hiccups and burps. The bewildered audience gave me a spattering of applause out of respect for my uniform, and I collapsed in a giggling heap at the side of the stage after my wobbly exit. It was a very sorry performance indeed, and Danny Williams told me the following day that I had let the whole regiment down, as indeed I had. It taught me a lesson I never forgot. Alcohol and performing don't really mix – at least, old and mild with a whisky chaser don't mix. Mind you, brandy on the other hand, taken in moderation. . .

I would have been far more careful about my performance had I realized that Joy's younger brother, a lad a couple of years my junior, was destined for a glittering future in the theatre, films and television. He was a quiet chap who, on one occasion, had carried my kitbag when he came with Joy to meet me at the station on my return from leave. He did it with that panache for which Donald Sinden was to become famous. For it was none other than he, gentle reader. A memory to cherish.

CHAPTER FIVE

The Real Thing

We stood at our boat stations on deck, fully equipped and wearing Mae West life jackets. It was customary for us to muster one hour before dawn and one hour before dusk just in case Jerry caught sight of our convoy. Johnny Owens from Tumble, for whom I had acted as best man at his wedding the previous year, leaned over the ship's rail and pointed to the line of snow-covered mountains tracing the horizon to the north of us.

'That's the Sierra Nevada, boyo,' he said.

'All things considered, I'd much rather be looking at Kilvey Hill,' I replied, reflecting the mood of all of us on board the *Stratheden*.

The ship was part of the great 'Operation Torch', the code name for the invasion of North Africa, and we were now well past Gibraltar. All around us, corvettes and frigates fussed over the passenger liners which now served as troop ships, signalling every so often in Morse code to each other. So far, we appeared not to have been spotted by the enemy – a fact I found unbelievable, such was the size of the convoy.

We had embarked at Greenock on 15 October 1942, completely unaware of our destination.

We knew, of course, that we were going to war, and for security reasons embarkation leave had been dispensed with. I was lucky enough to have been given ordinary leave on 27

September, and because of my work in the battery office I was able to intimate to my parents that I would not see them again for some time.

I vividly remember Mam and Dad coming to see me off from the old LMS station in Swansea. We chatted gaily on the platform before the train came in. The conversation was about important things like not catching cold and how well the Russians were fighting and how I was to take care of myself and about Carol's new boyfriend and about what we'd do at Christmas. And when the train did come in, my mother held me very close and Dad coughed and blew his nose on his handkerchief several times. As the train drew away from the platform I waved farewell, leaning as far out of the carriage window as I dared, watching them as they stood hand in hand, trying to smile as their son went off to war.

The regiment was no longer a second-line support unit, we were now part of the 78th Division. At the end of July 1942 we had moved up to Dunblane in Perthshire where we were completely re-equipped and reinforced up to strength. We were trained for assault landings, and 'loading and unloading of guns and vehicles were intensively practised on the Clyde', as the Regimental History states laconically. We were also taken out into the hills around Dunblane at night-time in closed trucks and ordered to make our way back to base with the aid of a prismatic compass. I wasn't too bad at this; I already had a very strong sense of survival and I had learned to find my way about pretty well. If anyone had to lead a retreat I was going to be the first one to volunteer.

There was now one gleaming stripe on my arm. I had achieved the highest rank I was ever to attain in the army, that of a lance-bombardier. I had been sent on a course to Edinburgh Castle in August so that I could become a fully-fledged army pay clerk. It was an easy task after the experience I already had and I came out top of the course, a fact which caused great merriment when I got back to the battery office.

'Come on, snap out of it.' Johnny Owens tugged my arm. 'Let's have a sing-song.'

This was always easy to arrange, especially as a lot of our original Welsh complement were still with the regiment. In no time at all the deck rang with the sound of three-part harmony as we sang ourselves through the Mediterranean night. Welsh songs, rugby songs, songs that were unrepeatable in polite society, and lastly, hymns, which have always been my favourite kind of music. Then the inevitable 'Come on now, lads, break it up. You'll wake the bloody Jerry submarines,' from someone in authority, and we'd break off reluctantly and shuffle our way back down to the hammocks that were our sleeping accommodation between decks. Back to the smell of sweat and fear, and our own thoughts.

Ten days out at sea we were informed of our destination, and for some reason the knowledge of where we were going removed some of the foreboding we had felt. In the army it was always the fear of the unknown that was hardest to take; once a task was made clear it was somehow more bearable, however hard it might be. We also heard over the ship's tannoy system of the great victory at El Alamein and that cheered us up no end. Between us – the First and the Eighth armies – we'd soon have Jerry bottled up. We thought like that then.

Our part of the convoy, the second echelon, as we were called, landed a couple of days after the rest of the regiment. We came ashore at Algiers without incident and I was greatly excited by the sights and smells of the place. There was one particular aroma which I always associate with Algiers and that was the gas they used to power the cars and lorries. There was a great shortage of petrol and all the vehicles seemed to carry large gas containers on their roofs. It smelled like rotten apples, but was not exactly unpleasant. However, there were also plenty of pongs of the unpleasant kind about.

The political situation was uncertain for a while and the guns were deployed on the golf course all set to fire on Fort L'Empereur where Darlan, the head of state in French Africa, was rumoured to be in hiding. Nothing came of it, however, and we sat around waiting for our next move. It was not long in coming. It was decided on 15 November that 11th Infantry Brigade, with our regiment in support, was to head for Tunis, five hundred miles away.

My duties, apart from being a command post officer's assistant and pay clerk, now included riding a motor cycle as a relief despatch rider, and I was called upon to ride MC 13, a 500 cc Norton, all the way from just outside Algiers to our ultimate destination in Tunisia. It was a hair-raising and backside-bruising journey that included hairpin bends and long stretches of badly maintained roads. On occasions, because I spoke fairly reasonable French, I was sent on ahead with Lieutenant John Booth as a pillion passenger to arrange billets for the regiment.

We were generally the first British soldiers that the local inhabitants had seen, and in one small town near the Tunisian border we were fêted by the mayor on the town hall steps. Johnny Booth and I stood and toasted 'La France' and 'L'Angleterre' in glasses of some potent anisette which were presented to us on a silver tray, and we were offered the freedom of the town hall. It was decided that we needed somewhere a little less grand in which to billet the troops, and settled finally for a tobacco factory on the outskirts of the town.

The following morning I had a monumental headache and every bump in the road sent shock waves of pain up the back of my neck. But it wasn't long before the sheer exhilaration of being part of an advancing army took over. We were heading, it transpired, for a town called Medjez-el-Bab, where we had been ordered to secure the bridge over the Medjerda River. This little white Arab town was the gateway to the valley that led to Tunis, and we were to see a lot of it before the campaign was over.

When we eventually reached Medjez-el-Bab the excitement had begun to wear off, at least it had as far as I was concerned. We had been subjected to enemy attacks from the air ever

My father, Frederick Ernest Secombe (*above left*) during the
First World War, and (*above right*), Grandpa Secombe.

Grandpa Secombe with my mother.

With my elder brother, Fred, in 1924, wearing my father's tie.

As a twelve-year-old choirboy.

Seated, third from right, at St Thomas' Boys Elementary School, Swansea.

My sister, Carol.

Age 14, with Carol.

With Carol in the
Welsh Courtship act.

Form A.

CENTRAL

WELSH BOARD

SCHOOL CERTIFICATE EXAMINATION

This is to certify that:

I. *Harry Donald Secombe* _____

_____ born *September 8 1921*

attended the following Secondary Schools:

 the Dynevor Secondary School from *September* ___ 1933 to *July* ___ 1937

and ___ from ___ 19 ___ to ___ 19 ___

and pursued a Course of Study in the subjects enumerated on the back of this Certificate.

Llewelyn John   Head ~~Mistress~~ Master.

and that having been examined in the following Groups of Subjects :

    (i) ENGLISH SUBJECTS,
    (ii) LANGUAGES,
    (iii) SCIENCE AND MATHEMATICS,
    (iv) OTHER SUBJECTS,

II. (*s*)he passed the School Certificate Examination of the Central Welsh Board in *July* ___ 1937, passing with Credit in the following subjects: *English ; French (Written and Oral), German (Written and Oral); and Art* ___

Signed on behalf of the Central Welsh Board.

_____
    Chairman.

and that

III. The Board of Education have inspected the School(*s*) and recognized it ~~them~~ as (an) efficient Secondary School(*s*), and accept the Examination as reaching the approved standard and as being suitable for the ~~last-named~~ School.

Signed on behalf of the Board of Education.

W. P. Wheldon
Permanent Secretary to the
Welsh Department.

My School Certificate, 1937.

As Lance-Bombardier Secombe in the army in Italy in 1945.

In the army, 1943.

Welcome home from St Barnabas Church.

Saint Barnabas 1939 1945 Parish Church

Swansea

Presented to *Harry D. Secombe*

It is with a profound sense of Thankfulness and Gratitude that the Church extends to you a cordial Welcome on returning home safely from the perils and hazards of the World War, being deeply conscious of the grave dangers and hardships you had to endure whether serving on Sea, Land, or in the Air.

The Thoughts and Prayers of your Church have always been a constant petition for your protection and well-being, believing that your Loyalty, Fortitude and Sacrifice will enable future generations to live in peace and security.

May the remainder of your life be blessed with every Happiness.

On behalf of the Church,

Dr Luther Thomas
Vicar.

Out of uniform at last.

since we had crossed the mountain range which marked the Algerian/Tunisian border. By this time the Germans were pouring men and equipment into Tunisia by sea and by road from Tripolitania – but nobody had told me that. Our supplies had to come from the Bône which was seized early on and made safe for shipping, but the port was bombed so heavily and consistently day and night that there was no Arab labour to unload the ammunition and petrol, and so the lads had to do it themselves.

The regiment went into action on the night of 24 November in support of the three infantry battalions which made up the 11th Brigade – the 2nd Lancashire Fusiliers, the First East Surreys and the 5th Northants – who went into the attack the following day. Unfortunately the attack failed after coming under heavy machine and field gunfire, the Fusiliers' CO, Colonel Manly, being killed as they approached the river.

It was in this engagement that our regiment got its first MC. Captain Barker-Benfield, who was forward observation officer, managed to cross the breast-high river with a wireless set strapped to his back and brought fire down on the machine gun posts, enabling the Fusiliers to withdraw.

On the next day, when the Brigade attacked again, Medjez was found to be empty of German troops, and though the vital bridge had been blown, our engineers started building a hundred-foot span bridge – their first in action – and there it remained for the rest of the campaign. There were rumours later on that one of the engineers had 'sold' it to an Arab entrepreneur who began charging vehicles a toll to cross the bridge.

The next move as far as I was concerned was on the 28th, when we left Medjez and headed for Smedia Farm, a large, prosperous farm about five miles to the north. I kept an intermittent diary at this time and as it's the only means I have of recollecting what happened, here are the entries for 28 and 29 November 1942:

'28th: Left Medjez for Smedia Farm. "B" Troop went forward to Tebourba. Dive bombed and 2 killed. BHQ left for Tebourba.

'29th: Arrived early morning. Started to dig slit trenches at once – till daybreak. Command Post set up in cactus grove. "A" Troop in anti-tank role in strip of wood on main road just outside Tebourba in front of Command Post. Rather severe air attacks in early afternoon. One Stuka shot down by Lt anti-aircraft guns.'

Earlier, on the 27th, our sister battery, 322, which was supporting the East Surreys, was attacked at mid-morning by seventeen tanks at close range. Our gunners knocked out fourteen of them, and at the end of the day seven out of 322's eight guns had been put out of action. The one remaining gun had been manned by Sergeant Busty Eustace on his own, 'and the knocked-out ranks formed a ring around the battery, one of them only three yards from the muzzle of the gun that had destroyed it.' (The quote is from the book about the 78th Division, *From Algiers to Austria* by Cyril Ray.)

Sergeant Eustace won the DCM, and my old mate Signaller Dixie Deans got the MM for keeping up communications throughout the battle from an unarmoured truck.

The next few days from 30 November to 3 December were sheer hell for everybody. Dive-bombers and tanks had almost wiped out 496 Battery with a high percentage of officers and men being killed and wounded.

Our Battery, commanded by a very brave Major Giles Brocklebank who was awarded the MC for his part in the battle, was now in the thick of things. I had dug myself a slit trench which not only went straight down several feet, but also went lengthwise. 'One more inch, Secombe,' said the Sergeant-Major, and I'll charge you with desertion.'

I remember going to obey a call of nature during a lull in the battle, taking with me a shovel as we were required to do. As

I was fearfully carrying out my duty in a squatting position, I heard something whizz past my right ear. When I looked behind me I saw that a bullet had punched a neat hole in a prickly pear cactus. My first instinct was to stand up and tell whoever had done it to be more careful, and then the realization crept over me that the person who had fired the shot had every intention of killing me. After I had scrambled back to my slit trench I was never the same carefree lad again.

As the battle progressed our position came under mortar fire from almost every direction, and then came the sound of tank fire. Major Brocklebank decided that he would try to find where the tanks were situated, and as I happened to be out of my slit trench at the time, he summoned me to accompany him. 'Put these in your battledress blouse,' he said, handing me two hand grenades. I had never really got on with hand grenades, and as we set off on our reconnaissance I was more afraid of them than I was of the Germans.

'Keep close behind me,' he said as we crawled on our bellies towards the crest of the hill behind BHQ.

The sweat was pouring down my face as I tried to stop the grenades from banging against each other inside my jacket.

Brocklebank beckoned sharply to me from his position just below the top of the hill. 'Look at that,' he said, pointing towards two large German tanks which were laying up, hull down, in a hollow on the other side of the crest.

I stared in sheer terror at the sight below, the big black crosses on the sides of the tanks leaping out at me. In the near distance a couple of British tanks were on fire and puffs of black smoke floated lazily into the air. It was like a scene from a film, but I was only too aware that there would be no interval with ice-cream and chocolates.

'Check my reading,' whispered the Battery Commander, handing me a prismatic compass which shook like a small blancmange in my hands. As I was reading off the scale, Brocklebank calmly took out his cigarette case and offered me a fag. I shook my head wordlessly. I just wanted to get back to the comparative safety of the Command Post. It was remarkable how degrees of danger shifted in one's mind in battle. Regimental Headquarters could seem like the front line when you first went into action, then when you went forward to the gun position you yearned for the security of RHQ, and the gun positions seemed like paradise when you were at the observation post with the infantry.

'Keep your distance on the way back,' said Brocklebank after he had smoked half his cigarette, which he pinched out and replaced in his case. I overtook him three times, the hand grenades clanking ominously under my blouse. When we finally got back to the command post and I had been relieved of my unwanted cargo, the major came over to where I was standing – outside my slit trench – and said 'Secombe, I think I left my cigarette case up on the ridge. Could you go and look for it for me?'

I don't know to this day whether or not he was joking but I went around the corner of the Arab huts in the cactus grove which formed our command post, stayed there out of sight for about ten minutes, and then reported that I could not find his case.

'Oh, all right,' said Brocklebank, rather too readily accepting the fact.

Another very courageous man was Bombardier Ken Harling, who in Civvy Street worked in the city. He was quite a bit older than the rest of us but when the chips were down, as they were in Tebourba, he showed absolutely no fear at all. He, too, was awarded the MM for his coolness in action, and was wounded by a mortar shell on the last day before we were forced to withdraw. When we got back to Smedia Farm after the battle I wrote a letter to his wife in Epsom. Here's part of it:

'I felt I must write to you to let you have some first-hand information of the whole incident, as Ken was my best friend – rather he was more like a brother than just a friend – and I know he would like me to tell you all I know.

'It happened on the afternoon of December 3rd when we were in action and were undergoing a rather fierce bombardment from the air and from gunfire. Ken, in his capacity as signal NCO, was out repairing a break in the line caused by a shell burst. Prior to this he had been manning a telephone and doing other routine jobs which in action take a lot of nerve to carry out. . .

'Unfortunately, however, a mortar shell landed some few yards away from him before he had time to take proper cover. He dropped forward on his face, saving most of the blast, but too late to stop three pieces of shrapnel which struck him – one in each arm and the other just above the knee. He managed to crawl into a slit trench and there his wounds were dressed by an officer. They were not very serious – just rather deep flesh wounds, but he lost quite a lot of blood from them.

'We got a stretcher for him and he was taken to our nearest dressing-station. Then came the worst part. We had orders to move from our own area, owing to heavy enemy pressure, and fight our way out. But because the dressing-station was some distance in front of our position, we were unable to evacuate all the wounded except those who could actually walk. Thus Ken, who had a leg wound, had to be left in the dressing-station with other casualties to await inevitable capture by the Germans. The doctor, however, stayed with his patients and you can rest assured that Ken was as comfortable as he could possibly be.

'Throughout the whole of the incident, especially when his wounds were being dressed, he displayed really marvellous courage – even to the extent of getting onto the stretcher himself. He smiled at me as he was carried away and said "I'll be all right, boy."

'. . .A spirit like Ken's will always be undaunted, whatever the circumstances.'

In the event Ken was not taken prisoner, but after a series
of bizarre accidents was ultimately evacuated by an American
half-track and in due course was invalided out of the army.

The evening of 3 December was a nightmare. We had been
firing open sights with all the ammunition we had left – smoke
shells and armour-piercing shells which were normally used
against tanks. The Hampshires had fought magnificently, one
of their officers, Major le Patourel, winning the VC, and
their strength had diminished to only ten officers and two
hundred men. Led by their CO, Colonel Lee, they cut their
way through Tebourba, firing their Bren guns from the hip.
Then came the order for all troops to withdraw, and it is a
credit to our Battery that we brought out what guns we had
left. What remained of the East Surreys came out with us.

I found myself clinging to the back of a three-ton truck,
while overhead the tracer bullets seemed to travel in slow mo-
tion. The Germans, fortunately, were not too sure about what
was happening, and most of us managed to reach the safety
of Smedia Farm back down the road towards Medjez-el-Bab.
Johnny Owens and I made the escape together, but some of
our lads were taken prisoner after we'd had an argument
about which track to take. They went one way and were
captured, Johnny and I went the other and survived. The
luck of the draw, I suppose.

Our brave bid to take Tunis quickly did not come off,
though we had come to the very brink of success. We failed
only because our force was too small. Nobody could ever say
that we didn't try. There could be no reproach.

Ask anyone who fought in the First Army in Tunisia what
his abiding memory of the campaign was – apart from the

Germans, of course – and he'll answer 'the mud'. Mud was everywhere, in our hair, in our food, and it plastered our uniforms like liquid cement. Tanks sank up to their turrets in it, and even when the surface of the ground dried out there was always three or four feet of oozy clay underneath.

The rain began in our sector on about 6 December, and it fell for three days and nights. There was no respite from it and no protection either. I had always imagined North Africa to be a hot, sandy place with oases and palm trees, but it soon became clear that the climate was more European than African. Down where the glamorous Eighth Army were fighting it was more like the popular conception of desert warfare, but where we were that December it might just have been Ystalyfera with Arabs.

We spent most of the month around the Medjez area, patrolling and waiting to be re-equipped and for reinforcements. The food we were getting was not too bad. It was called 'composite rations' officially, but we knew it as 'compo rations'. A box containing food for fourteen men for one day, it consisted of forty-two tinned meals, along with boiled sweets, cigarettes and, most importantly, toilet paper. The best combination was the box that held steak and kidney pudding, golden syrup sponge, and Players cigarettes. If you were unlucky you got McConochie's stew and soya links with Capstan full-strength. It also contained a tin of tea, sugar and dried milk all mixed up together. This concoction we would throw into water which we boiled in the tin in which the hard tack biscuits had been packed. I could never get used to the stuff, but most of the lads thrived on it, taking every opportunity to brew up.

The biscuit tins were very useful for collecting water and for boiling our lice-ridden underwear. They were also supposed to act as ovens when turned on their sides and punctured with holes to let out the steam. It certainly didn't work for Johnny Owens and myself that Christmas. We were billeted on a farm and I had managed to persuade the Arab farm manager to sell me a chicken for twenty cigarettes. He took the fags and handed over a live bird. Now, neither Johnny nor I had ever killed anything – not even Germans as far as we knew – but our desire to have a change of diet was stronger than our qualms and we set about slaughtering the poor creature with a machete. I'll draw a veil over the actual killing, except to say that I think it died from laughter at our attempts to despatch it.

Faced with the dead chicken, we began to prepare it for our dinner. First, we realized, it had to be plucked – and our clumsy efforts removed as much surface skin as feathers. Then there was the problem of cooking the damned thing. We started a fire with petrol-soaked wood in a circle of stones, placed the bird inside the biscuit tin, laid the tin on its side, duly peppered with holes as instructed, and sat back to await results. They say that a watched pot never boils – well, I can assure you that a watched chicken never cooks, at least ours didn't. We went off to collect some bottles of beer which had come up with the rations and supplemented them with a couple of mugfuls of our Christmas rum ration. Soon, a rosy glow came over us, which was more than could be said for the chicken. It just lay there, smoking. Eventually as evening approached and no fires were allowed after dark, we dragged the blackened corpse from the biscuit tin and tried to carve it. The stench was awful when we cut into it, and only then did we realize that you were supposed to take out the insides of poultry before cooking it. We had stew Christmas night and some more rum, and when the padre came along and asked me to lead a sing-song in the barn I couldn't even answer him.

There is only one entry for January in my diary for 1943:

'Friday, 1 January: Broke my glasses on way to Green Hill.'

JANUARY, 1943

MON.
4

TUES.
5

WED. *Epiphany* ● New Moon, **12.37** p.m.
6

Every effort has been made by the Publishers to obtain authentic information at the time of going to press. They cannot be held responsible for any errors or subsequent alterations.

The Moon's Phases throughout the Diary are Greenwich Mean Time, and are reproduced from the Nautical Almanac by permission of the Controller of H.M. Stationery Office.

THURS.
7

FRI. **JANUARY, 1943**
1 *New Year's Day*
Bank Holiday, Scotland
Broke my glasses on way to
Green Hill

FRI.
8

SAT.
2

SAT.
9

SUN. *2nd Sunday after Christmas*
3

SUN.
10 *1st Sunday after Epiphany*

10

11

Behind this brief sentence lies a story.

We were ordered up to the northern sector to support the Buffs of 36th Brigade in an attempt to take Green Hill, a dominating position ten miles short of Mateur. I know this now because I read it later on in the official history of the 78th Division. At the time I was only aware that I had to ride the dreaded MC 13, which was now a Matchless 350 cc, the Norton having been left behind somewhere in Tebourba. The mud was so bad that every few miles I had to undo the butterfly screws on the back mudguard and scoop out the liquid glue that clogged the wheel. Then I lost one of the screws in the stuff, and finally finding it after nearly a half-hour of searching, I kicked the starter so savagely that my glasses flew off and shattered on the petrol tank. I managed to make the rendezvous but my eyesight was so bad without my spectacles that I was useless for any duties other than carrying ammunition boxes and peeling spuds in the cookhouse. The attack failed – and we withdrew to positions near Medjez. Here it was decided that I was going to be a liability until I had a new pair of glasses, and I was duly sent off to the rear to get them.

For some reason I was officially classified as a 'walking wounded' and put on the ambulance train to Souk Ahras, back over the border in Algeria. I was issued with a brown label with my name, rank and number on it and told to report to the General Hospital. The journey back to base was very embarrassing because there were infantrymen with bullet and shrapnel wounds sharing the same compartment. I could not bear to tell them what was wrong with me, so I cultivated an air of mystery about myself, hinting at some obscure disease.

We arrived at Souk Ahras at night-time in the middle of an air raid, and things were pretty chaotic at the hospital. Those of us who could walk, shuffled in a line before a desk where our labels were taken from us. Then we sat around for a while as the bombs fell. When the all-clear went, an orderly summoned me, gave me a pair of pyjamas and told me to undress. I was in no position to question his orders, indeed I welcomed the chance of a kip in a real bed. 'This is the way the British Army looks after its lads,' I thought admiringly as I pulled the blankets over my head. My memory of the next few hours is hazy – I know I was awakened and given something to drink, and remember nothing more until I was shaken awake by a doctor in a white coat.

'How are you now, Brown?' he asked.

'Pardon, sir?' I tried to bring him into sharper focus by narrowing my eyes.

He repeated the question.

'My name is Secombe, sir. Lance-Bombardier 924378.' I knew that much.

The doctor looked at something tied to the foot of the bed. 'Aren't you Fusilier Brown?'

'No, sir.'

'Have you got dysentery, then?' The doctor was getting irritable by this time.

'No sir, I've broken my glasses,' I stammered.

'Get out of that bloody bed, man.' The MO was furious. 'Give him his uniform and send the bugger to the optician,' he said to the orderly with him.

As I dressed I learned that there had been a monumental mistake and that some poor fusilier had been up all night filling sandbags in between rushing to the latrines. Then, to cap it all, he'd been given an eye test, which must have seemed a strange treatment for what ailed him.

I was given pretty short shrift, and was provided with two new pairs of spectacles in no time at all. Secretly I had banked on having to wait a couple of days while they tried to fix me up with the strong lenses I required, but I had to be content with just the one night's bed and board. I don't know what was in the drink they gave me that night but it was nearly a week before I had a bowel movement – and it took a mortar attack to move me.

At the beginning of February we were once more in support of the 11th Infantry Brigade – the 2nd Lancashire Fusiliers, the 1st East Surreys and the 5th Northants – south of Medjez overlooking the Goubellat Plain. Battery Headquarters was set up in a farm and conditions became static for a week or two, with the wind and rain adding to our discomfort. A lot of spare time was spent trying to chip away the mud from our uniforms and equipment, because when the stuff dried it was like concrete. The Arabs made bricks out of it.

Then, according to my diary, on 27 February (which, incidentally, appears to be a day behind the official regimental history – but then I never knew what day it was when we were in action) we were attacked by a much bigger force and nearly over-run. My diary for that day says:

FEBRUARY, 1943	MARCH, 1943
MON. 22	**MON.** *St. David's Day* 1 lunch quicker — hell. Lt. in A.A. who knows Dewi Williams down south. Capt. Browne - Kenpie wore
TUES. 23	**TUES.** *Fairly quiet.* 2 Bag counted down South consisted of 2 Mk IVs 1 88 mm gun, 15 lorries and 3 staff cars !!!
WED. *St. Matthias* 24	**WED.** *Quiet during day. Lots of* 3 own planes in sky. Bit of misunderstanding between men and French infantry caused quite a flap!
THURS. 25	**THURS.** 4 lovely day — nothing much doing. Lot of banging down far South. Jerry plane down
FRI. 26	**FRI.** 5 Fairly quiet. Planes came over — ours + their bar morning in our area
SAT. ☾ Last Quarter, 6.22 p.m. 27 Party started at 4 o'clock in morning. Lasted throughout day with terrific casualties for Jerry. Capt. Reader + Newall killed by mine.	**SAT.** ● New Moon, 10.34 a.m. 6
SUN. *Sexagesima* 28 Battle continued on Plain but consisted mostly of small pockets lying up in gullies + nullahs.	**SUN.** *Quinquagesima* 7

19

'Party started at 4 o'clock in the morning. Lasted throughout day with terrific casualties for Jerry. Captain Reader and Newall killed by a mine.

'Saturday, 27 February: Battle continued on Plain but consisted of small pockets lying up in gullies and nullahs.

'Sunday, 28 February: Much quieter.

'Monday, 1 March, St David's Day Fairly quiet. Bag counted down south consisted of two Mk IV (tanks), one 88 mm gun, fifteen lorries and three staff cars.

'Tuesday, 2 March: Quiet during day. Lots of own planes in the sky. Bit of misunderstanding between own and French infantry caused quite a flap!

'Wednesday, 3 March: Lovely day – nothing much doing. Lot of banging down south. Jerry plane down.

'Thursday, 4 March: Fairly quiet. Planes came over – ours and his, but nothing in our area.'

Those few sentences conceal a hell of a battle with the 10th Panzer Division, the one that was the spearhead of the Germann Army in the smashing of France. Along with them were parachute troops and the Potsdam Grenadiers; altogether about forty-five thousand hardened fighting men. If only I'd known what we were up against, I would have set off for Algiers on MC 13, mud or no mud.

At the end of March, the regiment moved down into the Le Kef area to prepare for the big offensive which was to drive Von Arnim's army out of Africa. The weather was getting warmer and there were longer periods of sunshine between the rainstorms, so it was obvious to those in command – though not to me – that it was time to strike back.

Reinforcements were arriving all the time and on one particular occasion we were instructed to dig gun-pits for a detachment of 7.2 gun howitzers which had just come into the area. They were to be deployed on a plateau for the purpose of destroying some enemy gun positions which were sited in rock caves deep in the hillside.

We dug the gun-pits, as ordered, in the daytime and the guns moved in under the cover of darkness. I happened to be sitting in an eight-hundredweight wireless truck in a gully below a steep cliff which led up to the plateau where the guns were intended to come into action.

Meanwhile, up above us the big guns with their rubber tyres and huge barrels had been manhandled into position. It was the custom when artillery of this calibre was used, that the first round was fired by just one gun, using a rope attached to the firing mechanism. The gun was duly fired, but, owing to the fact that we had been given the wrong specifications, the gun-pit was too shallow to accommodate the recoil of the barrel. Consequently it bounced out of its pit and careered backwards over the cliff under which our little wireless truck was positioned.

The noise was quite terrifying and my first reaction was that if the enemy had now taken to firing entire guns at us and not just shells, it was about time we packed in the whole business. Nobody seemed to know exactly what had happened and because it was night-time, there was not much point in running about looking for trouble.

Suddenly the canvas flap of the truck was swept aside and a dim face appeared in the light of our paraffin lamp.

'Anybody seen a gun?' inquired the intruder.

'What colour?' we replied.

It was a certain Bombardier Milligan who was to play quite as prominent part in my life in the near future, but who was then, like myself, only playing 'walk-on' parts in battles. At the time I had no idea who he was, and it was only much later on in Italy, when we were discussing the North African campaign, that I realized it was he who had lost the gun.

On 7 April the division launched an attack which was designed to clear the hills to the north of Medjez; Djebel Ang and Tangoucha along with the Berber villages of Toukabeur Chaouach and the Heidous. When these were taken Medjez would be free from the possibility of counter-attack and the final battle for Tunis could begin. To give a flavour of what went on from our battery's point of view, here are some more extracts from my diary:

'Wednesday, 7 April: Fired at 0350 hours, heaviest barrage seen in Tunisia – 15,000 rounds. Moved forward after 2nd objective taken.

'Thursday, 8 April: Fired Y targets and U targets ['Yorker' targets required the three batteries to fire, i.e. the whole regiment of artillery, and 'Uncle' targets called for all the division's artillery] nearly all day. Osbourn killed at observation post. Very windy and slight rain. Eight Stukas shot down.

'Friday, 9 April: Discovered gun positions to be in mine-field. Recce of new locations prior to move, which later cancelled. Captain Browne gets MC.

'Saturday, 10 April: Move took place after all into hills behind Pt 667 [north of Chaouach village]. Arrived after dark and set up command post.

'Sunday, 11 April: No firing done. Two Stukas shot down. Battle going well so far.

'Tuesday, 13 April: Preparations all day for big barrage supporting attack by 11th and 36th brigades. Biggest load of shit going off at 2300 hours ever!

'Wednesday, 14 April: Took all objectives by tea-time with exception of Tangoucha. Not held in much strength. Fired Y and U targets.

'Thursday, 15 April: Jerry counter-attacked on Bou Diss. Driven off. Start day beating off counter-attacks. Still hold all ground. Barrage fired at night.

'Friday, 16 April: Captain Browne went into action with feet [infantry]. Injured. Guthrie and Chamberlain wounded. Attack unsuccessful. Situation remains unchanged.'

Although Tangoucha was still held by the enemy, Medjez was now free from attack and our ten-day battle had been a success. The division had taken 1,080 prisoners and the First Army Commander, General Anderson, wrote in his despatch: 'I consider that 78th Division deserves the highest praise for as tough and prolonged a bit of fighting as has ever been undertaken by the British soldier.'

The one hill which had been a thorn in the side of the British advance from the very beginning of the campaign was Longstop Hill, which dominated the Medjez to Tunis road. Until it was taken, the guns positioned on it could prevent any assault on Tunis. The Guards Brigade and the American combat team attached to our command had tried unsuccessfully to take it at Christmas. Now, on Thursday, 23 April, on the eve of Good Friday, it was the task of 36th Brigade – the Buffs, the Royal West Kents and the Argylls, along with the East Surreys and the tanks of the North Irish Horse – to take Longstop once and for all.

I have a vivid recollection of line after line of infantrymen moving up the slopes before us, silhouetted against the evening sky. The red poppies were out and a profusion of spring flowers carpeted the hills around, as these brave men walked silently upwards into their attack positions. We gunners could only stand in silent awe and admiration as we watched them go by our guns.

'Friday, 23 April: Infantry encountering fierce opposition on Longstop and Tangoucha. Fired barrage.

'Saturday, 24 April: Big final attack expected on Longstop and Tangoucha. Heidous evacuated by enemy.

'Sunday, 25 April: Fired lot of ammunition. Tangoucha taken. Most of Longstop in our hands.'

By the 26th all of Longstop had been taken and in the fighting leading up to its capture, Major Anderson of the 8th Argyll and Sutherland Highlanders won the VC.

On 29 April we were issued with khaki drill for the first time and we all shed our lousy battledress with whoops of delight. It had been getting warmer every day and the wool uniforms were becoming unbearable in the heat. White knees were exposed for the first time as we donned our new shorts, and we all had red 'V's where the sun had tanned our necks.

The battle for Tunisia was now virtually over for the division, although our regiment's twenty-five pounders were still in demand as we advanced along the Tunis road. On 3 May we met up for the first time with the Eighth Army. We were somewhat embarrassed by the newness of our uniforms and the whiteness of our knees, but in the face of their undoubted glamour and bronzed complexions we felt we had done at least as good a job as they had. When one of them shouted 'Get your knees brown' at me, my raspberry came into good use.

'Friday, 7 May: Moved in afternoon. Roads in bad condition and blocked with traffic. Tunis fallen!!

'Saturday, 8 May: Moved forward into area two miles from Tunis. Went through streets of Tunis and Carthage. Terrific response from people.'

That was a tremendous day, and none of us could stop smiling as our dust-covered trucks and guns bearing the yellow battleaxe insignia of the 78th Division crawled at a snail's pace through the packed streets of Tunis. We were cheered and pelted with flowers, and here and there German soldiers stood and watched us in bewilderment. The final advance had been so fast that we took several days to round up all the prisoners and take them to hastily prepared prison stockades.

There was a glorious moment on the beach near Carthage. The band of the Hermann Goering Jaeger Division had been captured, complete with instruments, and they sat on the sands in a roped-off enclosure, guarded by Redcaps. There they played selections from Strauss and 'Roll Out the Barrel' and 'Mademoiselle from Armentiers', while we all stood around in our drawers, cellular, short, clapping their efforts. We threw cigarettes in a couple of hats that the Redcaps had set down in the sand, and none of us could really believe it was happening.

It was a heady time for us and when we had settled down under canvas outside Carthage, we were allowed some time to ourselves. On the Monday after Tunis fell, Lieutenant Joe Cattermole, our Command Post Officer, and myself were driving around the back streets when we came across a huge green door. Joe, who had an inquisitive nature, naturally wanted to know what was behind it, though my own instinct was to leave well alone. It turned out that on the other side of the door were dozens of Jewish people who had been rounded up by the Germans and then left to their own devices as the battle for Tunis developed.

We were the first British soldiers they had seen, and they were pathetically grateful to us for saving them, although all we had done was open the door. In no time at all they dragged out tables and chairs into the courtyard of the place in which they had been incarcerated and produced bottles of anisette and sweet wine which they had hidden from the Germans. We were able to do some of them a favour by borrowing a three-ton truck from the battery vehicle park and moving them back into their homes again.

Lieutenant John Booth, who had ridden behind me on MC 13 to fix billets for the regiment when we first went into action, decided we should have a concert in the little George Metaxas Theatre in Tunis.

We got together those who could do a bit of a turn and I did my impressions, along with a parody to the tune of 'Waltzing Matilda' called 'Lost at Tebourba'. After the withdrawal from that unholy place, any piece of equipment missing from a kit inspection was deemed to have been lost at Tebourba. I can only remember the first verse, which went:

'Lost at Tebourba, lost at Tebourba,
Lost all my kit at Tebourba I did,
And they moaned and they sighed
As they went up to the quarter bloke,
Lost all my kit at Tebourba I did.'

After three weeks' rest we moved to a place called Guelma for a month's training. The area was infested with mosquitoes and on 6 June I finished up in hospital with a temperature of 102°F. Fortunately it wasn't malaria but sand-fly fever, and I was discharged from hospital on the 13th. Ten days later, after we had moved east to Hammamet, at the southern end of the Cap Bon peninsula, I had a narrow escape.

We were positioned in an olive grove which had previously been used as some kind of depot by the Italians. All about the place lay red oval plastic objects, looking for all the world like Easter eggs.

On the 23rd it was my turn to be in charge of the guard and consequently Bombardier Reed, the specialist with whom I shared a pup tent, had the job of erecting it. I had started the job by clearing away some of the 'Easter eggs' and was then called away to mount the guard. A few minutes later there was one hell of an explosion, and when I ran towards the cloud of black smoke I found Bombardier Reed with part of his leg blown away. He had kicked an 'Easter egg' to one side and it had exploded. None of us had realized that these pretty-looking toys were actually Italian hand grenades, and only a few minutes before, I had been casually throwing them to one side. Someone 'up there' must have been keeping an eye on me.

The big moment of our stay in Hammamet was the visit to the unit of General Montgomery. He came to welcome us as part of the Eighth Army, the First Army now being behind us.

He arrived in style, the great man, wearing his famous beret and carrying a fly whisk, and sitting in the back of an open staff car. We were all standing to attention in a three-sided square when his car came to a halt in the middle of us.

He stood up and called, 'Bweak wanks and gather wound.'

Willy-nilly I was propelled forward by the press of the ranks behind me, and I found myself immediately beneath him, hard up against one of the rear wheels.

He looked around at us all and then said, 'Take your hats off, I want to see what you chaps look like.'

Now, I wasn't looking too good at this particular time. For one thing I had just had sand-fly fever, and I had also developed a fine crop of shiny boils; my glasses had been repaired with black tape – although I still had a spare pair in my kitbag – and under my beret, my hair had grown long. So it was with much trepidation that I complied with this illustrious general's command. My sand-coated hair fell over my face, and I was conscious of not looking my best as I lifted up my head.

Monty took his time reviewing his new acquisitions, nodding approvingly as his gaze swept around the assembly. And then he looked down and caught sight of me. He gave a kind of start of disbelief, then went on with his pep talk about 'hitting the Hun for six' and what a good job we'd done. And every so often his eyes drilled down in my direction.

I felt impelled to say something – 'I've been ill, sir' or 'I'll get my hair cut tomorrow, sir'. Instead, when there was a tiny lull in his speech, I called, 'We're with you, sir.'

He looked down at me once more for quite a few seconds, shook his head slightly and said, 'Ye-es,' without much conviction. Then he spoke a few more words and drove away, waving his fly whisk. I must have reminded him of Wellington's words after a march past of his troops before the Battle of Waterloo: 'I don't know what effect these men will have upon the enemy, but, by God, they terrify me.'

CHAPTER SIX

Italy – Shells and Showbiz

We knew that the advent of Montgomery meant that another invasion was imminent, and on 10 July, Sicily was the target.

Shortly afterwards we embarked at Sousse in tank landing-craft and two days later we came ashore at Syracuse. Our route took us north, through olive groves and vineyards, over very rough roads towards our rendezvous with the Canadians at a place called Catenanuova. In Tunisia we had had liquid mud to contend with; here we had dust, white and choking, which turned us all prematurely grey and got into everything we ate and everything we wore. It even filtered through the handkerchiefs we tied around our faces when we were on the move.

After we had taken Catenanuova, the division's next task was to remove the Germans from Centuripe, a fortress town on a jagged mountain ridge. It was a bit like the Gibb's Dentifrice Castle which used to be pictured on the toothpaste adverts, and it was held by a very tough bunch of lads – the Hermann Goering Division and the 3rd Parachute Regiment. According to captured documents, Centuripe was the pivot of the German defence strategy, and the resulting battle was as hard as anything we had encountered in Tunisia.

The attack began at first light on 31 July, twenty-four hours ahead of schedule, and continued until 3 August when the Royal Irish Fusiliers of the 38th Brigade broke through the town. It was a remarkable feat of arms, and though the gunners had to manhandle their guns over jagged lava beds, the victory belonged to the infantry.

My diary entries are very brief for this period – I must have been too busy carrying ammunition or trying to dig my way underground to find time for making notes.

'Wednesday, 4 August: Went through Centuripe. Awful place.

'Thursday, 5 August: Catania falls!

'Friday, 6 August: Adrano taken. Regiment moves up towards Bronte.

'Saturday, 7 August: Heard multiple mortar. Very shaken as usual.'

The sound of this multi-barrelled mortar – the nebel-werfer – was absolutely terrifying, and had me looking through my German – English dictionary for 'I'm on your side'. Later on it proved to be pretty inaccurate, but I never got used to the sound of the thing, and I don't think anyone else did either.

Bronte proved a hard nut to crack because it was on the lowest slopes of Etna's lava fields and there was only one single-way road into the town. We had to break down stone walls to get the guns into position, and in some cases fired from the road itself. However, on the afternoon of 8 August – the 7th Sunday after Trinity, as my diary tells me – the infantry of our 11th Brigade took the town. Incidentally, I found out from Joe Cattermole that Nelson had been made Duke of Bronte, and as far as I was concerned he was more than welcome to the place.

Randazzo was the next objective, and Jerry made his last stand in the area because the roads and the country were so difficult that advancing was a slow business. We were now moving around the western side of the massive Mount Etna towards the north, and ultimately Messina.

By 13 August Randazzo was taken and we met up with the Americans for the first time. Our division's engineers and the American infantry entered the town together, but there were no Germans left. When we went through there a couple of days later, not one building in the place was left standing, and the town had a population of ten thousand. The devastation was tremendous, worse than anything we had seen in Africa.

On Monday, 16 August we came out of action and my faithful diary records that on Wednesday, 18 August, I left to join the Divisional Concert Party.

We were a fairly mixed bunch of amateur performers gathered from units within the Division. There was a tall, melancholy chap called Garth who did female impersonations with two saucepan lids for a bust; a baritone, whose name escapes me; another lad called Robertson who did a comic vicar turn; a funny little comedian from a Field Ambulance Unit called Shorty Howard, who was very good, and – more importantly for me – Len Lightowler from 322 Battery of my regiment, who was the pianist for the show. A smiling, thick-set Yorkshireman, he was to become my accompanist and personal manager later on in my career. The party was commanded by Lieutenant Bracken of 56 Reconnaissance, who did monologues.

Our stage was a three-ton truck which had been adapted for the purpose, and for spotlights we had to use the headlights of another truck which carried all our personal gear. On the sides of the lorry ran the legend 'The Sicily Billies – Lava Come Back To Me'.

For our opening ensemble number Garth had written special words to Gershwin's 'Rhapsody In Blue', and – God forgive us – it went something like this:

'We come to you from out of the blue-oo,
With something to entertain-ain you-oo,
Give you a song to help to cheer you along
When you feel rather blue-oo.'

And it went downhill from then on. However, the audiences
had been so starved of entertainment for the past few weeks
that they laughed and applauded our efforts as if we had been
a West End revue company.

It was my first experience of doing an act night after night
and performing little sketches, and I began to feel like a
real professional. We lived like gypsies, driving around the
divisional area to give performances wherever the troops
happened to be. Sometimes the audience would contain local peasants who sat mystified throughout, and would only
laugh when Lieutenant Bracken came on to do his serious
monologue.

We had a great time swanning around the Sicilian countryside, drinking the dark local wine which we collected in
jerricans and which was apt to take the enamel off your
teeth. There were luscious grapes the size of plums hanging
in the vineyards, and we picked them greedily until we found
that some of the best bunches had been booby-trapped by
the retreating Germans. We chatted up the local girls, but
there was no chance of romance with any of them – there
was always a brooding relation lurking in the background to
make sure there was no hanky-panky.

The party broke up on 16 September, and I returned to the
regiment prior to our move to Italy. The Italians had already
surrendered and when we landed on 20 September at Reggio
di Calabra after a short trip from Messina, we all thought we'd
have a walk-over. We travelled in convoy across the foot of
Italy through glorious scenery until we got to Bari, where we
were billeted for a while on the outskirts of the city.

Entertaining fellow
soldiers in Italy,
1944-5. Fairy
queen – fair enough.

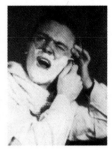

Shaving for a living at the Windmill Theatre,
October 1946.

With Jimmy Edwards at a *Weekly Sporting Review* party
and (*left to right*), a pretty lady, self, Johnny Mulgrew and
Leslie Welch, the 'Memory Man' (who would know the
name of the pretty lady).

Courting days, with Myra Atherton, 1946.

Myra, before our engagement.

'Resting' in digs.

Picture of a desperate second-spot comedian on tour.

Matinée idol.

One afternoon Johnny Owens and I were discussing the meal we'd most like to have when we had the chance, and we decided that roast chicken and chips would be favourite. The nearest we had come to it was the disastrous Christmas dinner in North Africa.

We had leave to go into Bari that day, and after sauntering through the streets, marvelling at the cheapness of the watches on display, we found a posh restaurant and marched inside. We must have looked a villainous pair, tin-helmeted and dusty, with our rifles slung over our shoulders. The tables were laid with white napkins and gleaming cutlery, and a bow-tied waiter approached us nervously. Neither of us spoke any Italian, but Johnny took it upon himself to explain what we wanted. He clucked like a hen and waved his arms in the air. The waiter backed away from him fearfully.

'Now do an impression of chips,' I said helpfully.

Between us we managed to make the waiter understand that we were not dangerous lunatics, but just two hungry squaddies in search of a good meal. He told us to come back in a couple of hours, and though we thought that we'd return to find the place bolted and barred, the dish we had longed for was waiting for us.

It was a sight to cherish – a whole roasted chicken on a silver dish, surrounded by a pile of chipped potatoes just as we'd ordered. We sat down and polished it off, helping it down with glasses of beer. We paid in British Occupation money, which caused the waiter's face to drop considerably, but when we threw in all the cigarettes we had on us, he managed a wan smile. I have to say that I've never tasted anything as delicious as that chicken – months of compo rations had dulled my taste buds and they had had a sudden glorious reawakening. Johnny and I returned to our olive grove, burping and patting our bellies in sheer contentment.

This feeling of goodwill stayed with me as we eventually headed north towards the coastal town of Termoli. I was riding MC 13 as usual, and as we went through some of the little towns on the way we were greeted like conquering heroes by the local inhabitants. After all, they were out of the war now. As we entered one town some miles out of Bari, I think it was called Cerignola, I had to sit on my bike and make sure that the convoy took the right road. People were throwing fruit and flowers to the soldiers in the trucks, and not wishing to miss out, I held out a hand to a dark-eyed beauty across the road from where I sat. She smiled and threw a pomegranate at me with such force that it knocked my goggles off and sent me flying off the bike. She then disappeared into the tittering crowd. It must have been an omen of some kind, because shortly afterwards we were strafed from the air.

I found myself cowering in a gully with a couple of lads from REME. "Ere,' said one of them. 'Wasn't you in that concert party?'

I nodded, keeping my face close to the ground.

'Sing us a song, then,' he said, as the planes wheeled overhead.

'Bugger off,' I said.

When we reached Termoli it was soon obvious that Jerry was going to make a stand and that our comparatively easy run up the coast road was over. The rain came early and hampered movement south of the Biturno River where the bridge leading into Termoli had been blown up. Some of the 11th Brigade crossed the river into the town in small craft, but most of us, including our battery, were still on the south side. Commandos had landed by sea to the north, but what we did not know was that the 16th Panzer Division were racing towards Termoli with orders to retake the town.

The battle raged for three days and in the fighting Major Anderson of the Argylls, who had won the VC at Longstop Hill, was killed at the brickworks to the west of the town. One of our officers, Captain Jim Gilburtson, got the MC here. He had gone ahead as forward observation officer and had found himself fighting along with the infantry.

By nightfall on 6 October the battle was over, and on the 9th I was sent back to Rear HQ to go to Tunis with a small party to collect the baggage the Division had left behind in Tunis. I welcomed my new orders with a joyful heart. All the fighting had affected my nerves, and it was an act of compassion on the part of Major Dennis Carey, our Battery Commander, to include me in the baggage detachment. It took us a week to get back to Tunis, because we had to hitch-hike our way from Taranto on an infantry landing-craft going to Syracuse. From there we boarded a French boat bound for Malta, arriving on the 23rd. We were not allowed to go ashore, so we stood on the deck of our somewhat battered boat, waiting for our next lift.

All around us in Valletta harbour there were sleek naval vessels. The officer in charge of us, a morose man, suddenly bucked up when he saw an Aldis lamp on board the battleship HMS *Rodney* signalling in our direction.

'Just a minute, chaps,' he said, stopping a noisy argument which had arisen about who could spit the furthest over the rail. 'It's a message about us.' He was a signals officer, so naturally he could read the message which was being sent in Morse code. 'Apparently we're to be picked up and taken on board this evening for the trip to Bizerta.' His back straightened and his face brightened. 'It's a rare honour for the Royal Navy to offer us a lift, especially in such a grand ship as the *Rodney*.' He looked at his scruffy command lolling about the deck. 'Get yourselves spruced up, chaps. We represent the 78th Division.'

We all went down below and cleaned ourselves up as much as we could and returned on deck to be met by our officer, resplendent in his best battledress jacket from which one pip had been removed on either epaulette. He had obviously been recently demoted from captain to lieutenant.

We stood around for a couple of hours, and then a naval officer came aboard our boat carrying some documents. Our officer advanced, smiling, and saluted smartly. 'Are you the party for Bizerta?' asked the naval bloke.

'That's right, and we're all very grateful for the honour you're doing us.'

'It's not much of an honour, mate,' replied the RN officer. 'Those LSTs roll something shocking when they're empty.'

'But what about our going on board the *Rodney*?' Our lieutenant was querulous now.

'*Rodney*? What do you mean?'

We explained that we had seen the Aldis lamp on the *Rodney* sending the message to our ship.

The navy man laughed. 'Oh, I see. That was the *Rodney* doing a favour for the tank landing-craft that'll be taking you on to Bizerta. It was passing on the message by Aldis because your bloke's out of sight around the harbour.'

Our lieutenant seemed to crumple, and shortly afterwards he went below to get drunk. As for us, we resumed our spitting competition over the rail until they came to transfer us to the LST.

Our sojourn in Tunis took quite a few weeks as we tried to trace the whereabouts of the contents of some of the kitbags. The store had been broken into and there were quite a few Arabs walking around wearing Sam Browne belts and sporting officers' shoes. We all felt deeply embarrassed at the comparatively small amount of kit we had to take back with us to Italy, but there was nothing we could do about it.

We eventually returned to the division in late December, and I found our battery in Vinchiaturo, where the snow lay deep over everything. My first job was to get stuck into helping to clear the blocked roads, and after the balmy air of Tunis I found the bitter cold hard to bear.

On 6 January we were off up the Adriatic coast and on the 8th we arrived at Casola. My diary for that day reads:

'Saturday, 8 January: Reported sick to MO in Casola. Twenty miles in open jeep in the snow. Arrived with temperature of 101. No ruddy wonder.'

It transpired that I had developed an inflammation of the gall bladder and kidneys, and after being transferred to the New Zealand Division Casualty Clearing Station at Vasto, I was eventually evacuated in an ambulance train to the 76th General Hospital in Trani.

Termoli was the last battle in which I was to take any part, and I was not to rejoin my regiment again. It was a fine unit, and I was proud to have been one of its members. 132 Field Regiment was home to me for four years, and I could not have grown up with a better bunch of lads.

We left a lot of our comrades lying under the ground in Tunisia and Sicily, and the regiment was to go on gathering glory in the slow slog up through Italy, finally finishing up in Austria. Those of us who are still left have a regimental reunion as often as we can, and we greet each other like brothers.

I spent five weeks in 76th General Hospital and lost about two stones in weight. At the end of my stay I was admitted to 11th Convalescent Depot just up the road from the hospital in Trani. It was a large Italian Army barracks and had a cinema which also doubled as a theatre. After I had parked my kit on the bunk bed allotted to me, I set out to find if there was a concert party associated with the theatre. To my delight there was a notice outside the cinema asking for volunteers for a variety concert that night. I gave my name to the sergeant in charge, Brian Sherman, and was given a spot on the show.

Fortunately my act went well and I became enrolled on the semi-permanent staff as a member of the concert party. It was a much more professional set-up than the divisional concert party had been. We had a band which was led by Brian Sherman, who also did the vocals, and there were some good entertainers among the group. One of them was a young lad who had been an actor before being called up. His name was Tommy Thompson, and as well as doing excerpts from Shakespeare, he did a very funny take-off of the Inkspots singing 'Whispering Grass'. He had been through a bad time as an infantryman and drank more than he should, but he was a great companion. Another member of the cast was Harold Nightingale who compèred the show and told some good stories. Later he was to become famous as the umpire who fell asleep during a televised tennis match at Wimbledon. There was a Belgian lad, Alan Van Houtem, who played the clarinet and was the scourge of all the ladies in the camp, and a fellow Welshman, Ivor Williams, who had a very fine baritone voice.

Ivor was an amazing character who was forever thinking up schemes to make money. One of his favourite methods was to buy a cheap, flashy watch in the town and then raffle it in the camp. There were lots of Yugoslav soldiers at the depot convalescing from wounds, and they loved to gamble. They were also fiery-tempered, and when one of them won a watch that stopped shortly after he had strapped it on his wrist, he chased poor Ivor all over the camp with a nasty-looking knife. However, Ivor's Welsh charm won the Yugoslav over, although it did cost him another watch.

The concert party became quite well known in the area and we began to perform for other units. My diary states:

'Friday, 10 March 1944: We did show at Barlatta Garrison Theatre. Not very big audience but very appreciative.

'Saturday, 11 March: Bigger audience tonight. Show went down terrific [sic]. Left for Bari at night for "Services Cocktail". Slept in Caruso's room.'

The last sentence referred to the dressing-room once used by Caruso in the huge Petruzelli Opera House in Bari, where I had been invited to perform in an all-services concert. According to my entry for the following day, the two performances went down well and the RAF Command Band wanted me as a compère. However, that must have fallen through, because on the following Monday, my diary entry reads:

'Arrived back at dinner-time from Bari wet through and a little fed up. Still – experience, old cock, experience.'

I settled down into a nice steady routine with the concert party. Every Sunday we did a show at the Eighth Army Rest Camp just outside Bari, where the troops came out of the line for a few days' rest. The experience of playing to different audiences was invaluable and I became convinced that when the war was over I was definitely going on the stage.

One morning Ivor and I saw our names in the Forces newspaper, *The Union Jack*. We were asked to report to Bari for a special 'Services Cocktail' show with Carroll Levis, the famous talent spotter.

'Saturday, 6 May: Left for Bari at 5 o'clock. Got lift on train with Sikhs and arrived just in time for rehearsal of broadcast.

'Sunday, 7 May: Broadcast with Carroll Levis in "Services Cocktail". Fame at last. Ha-ha.'

Carroll Levis appeared to have been impressed with my work and asked me to look him up when the war was over. He must have said that to lots of budding comics, but when I did get in touch with him after the war he put me in one of his 'Discovery' programmes as a 'star from the services'. It was to be my very first BBC broadcast.

Nothing spectacular happened for a few months apart from the fact that I caught malaria and had to go back to the 76th General Hospital for treatment. I had met an American GI in Bari called Joe Allen who was running the USO shows down there, and he gave me the odd date or two working American Air Force bases. It was a salutary experience because nobody seemed to listen to what I was saying. To be honest, I don't think they understood what the hell I was talking about in my Welsh-accented speech, which got faster and more incoherent in pace with my nervousness. However, Joe seemed satisfied and was quite content to pay me a few hundred lire for my pains.

All was going well until one day I returned from one of my jaunts to find the depot buzzing with rumours of a big clean-out. The comanding officer had been posted elsewhere and all superfluous personnel were to be sent back up the line. I was given a medical check-up and though I was not a hundred percent fit I was told to report to the Royal Artillery Training Depot at Eboli, which was across the other side of Italy from Trani, near Salerno. I had made many friends in the camp and quite a few friends in Trani itself. Alan Van Houtem and I had long been chatting up two eminently respectable and extremely well-chaperoned young sisters, Bianca and Teresa. Their father was a doctor and their brother a lieutenant in the Italian Army, and they had a cook who made wonderful pasta dishes. She was the one we were going to miss.

I arrived wet and miserable at Eboli some time in November – my diary holds no more entries. The place was a vast tented camp on the side of a hill and at first sight seemed very unpromising. Then I found that the depot boasted an extremely well-equipped theatre and that it had a permanent concert party of almost professional standard. I was allotted a place in a bell-tent under the supervision of a Bombardier Ticehurst, who had seen me perform back at the Eighth Army Rest Camp. He made some enquiries for me and arranged for me to meet Lieutenants Langston and Laurie Turner, the officers in charge of entertainment for the depot.

They didn't hold auditions, they put on a sort of 'talent night' concert every week, and I was put down as an entrant.

I was determined to do my best that night and I gave them all I'd got. Fortunately I was well received and I was offered a place in the regular show. Christmas was not far off – a big revue was being planned, and I was going to be given plenty to do.

For the time being I was to stay in the tent to which I had been first detailed, and later I was to move to a bigger tent in which all the regulars were billeted. I couldn't wait to move, because the tent in which I was sleeping also contained four amateur magicians, three of whom specialized in card tricks. The other was an illusionist called Max who spent all his time constructing a wooden lamp-post which kept collapsing on him. As far as the other three were concerned, I was the only one they could practise on.

I can see the tent now. The rain drumming on the canvas and a thin trickle of water gradually becoming a stream as it flows down the slope between the beds. A paraffin lamp swinging from its mooring place on the centre pole; in its dim light I am being exhorted to 'Take a card' by three eager lunatics, while in the background Max groans as his lamp-post falls down on him for the umpteenth time.

When the NAAFI closed I would wander about in the rain rather than return to the tent and be told, 'Shuffle the pack well; now cut them, and the next card you turn up should be the ten of clubs. Ah – now, just a minute. Something's gone wrong 'ere.' I was saved from pneumonia only by the departure from the concert party tent of a vocalist who had sung out of tune once too often.

The occupants of the 'show' tent were a motley crew, and I was surprised how untidy it was. The other tents in the camp were inspected every morning, but because the Camp Commandant, Major Derek Attwood, had a soft spot for 'theatricals', our tent was left alone.

It was here, in this tent, that an event occurred that was to have a profound effect on my future career. The audiences to whom we played demanded new material as often as possible, and it was essential that we changed our acts before the lads got fed up with them. By the time I had been there a few weeks, in spite of getting a good reaction from playing the

Fairy Queen in the pantomime, I was beginning to scrape the bottom of the not terribly deep barrel of my impersonations. The competition within the regular show was fierce, and if I didn't come up with something soon there was a real danger that I would have to go back up the line again – a prospect I did not relish at all.

The morning before my next scheduled performance, I was still desperately trying to think of something different to do in the act. I was shaving in a mirror attached to the tent pole, watched by a couple of the lads. One of them, Bombardier Sammy Lambert, was in charge of the tent's discipline, such as it was. He was a professional musician and before the war had been a saxophone player with Sid Dean's Band in Brighton.

'Come on, Secombe, hurry up,' he said, 'I want to use that mirror.'

I was slowly lathering my face at the time, still lost in thought about getting together some new material, and when Sammy gave me the 'hurry-up' I began to shave at a maniacal speed, covering myself in lather as I did so. Bill Hall, a magnificent violinist, but as eccentric as they come and a notoriously bad audience, was lying on the bed next to Sammy. He burst into laughter at my antics, and I suddenly realized that I had the beginnings of a new act.

When I had eventually dried myself off I went up into the hills behind the camp with a pad and pencil and worked out the basis of an act which was to launch me into the variety theatre and enable me to bring up a family.

It was quite simple, but nobody else seemed to have thought of the idea. All I did was to demonstrate the way different people shaved. First was a small boy playing about with his father's shaving gear, then came a soldier doing his ablutions in a bucket of ice-cold water with a blunt blade – all the lads appreciated that one – and I finished with an impression of a person who became embarrassed at being observed while shaving, which required me to drink the soapy water from the mug I'd been using. That was all there was to it, and I closed with my version of Jeanette MacDonald and Nelson

Eddy singing 'Sweethearts' as a duet – which included a fruity raspberry.

I began to use the raspberry as a device, blowing one every time I told a joke, and saying 'I was first!' It was really a desperate attempt to give myself the bird before the audience did, and in most cases it worked.

With this material behind me – can you believe this? – I became the principal comedian in the RATD show, and I was safe from being transferred back into action.

It was a very good place in which to learn the serious business of comedy. The theatre itself was run by Les Dodds who had been stage-manager at Wolverhampton's Grand Theatre, and he made us all behave like professional actors. A very clever Geordie named Harold Major wrote West End-standard revue sketches, and the music was written by Tony Thompson, a wild-eyed pianist who was a great enthusiast. Other members of the company were Haile and Beatty, two inseparable lads who were hysterically funny as a couple of NAAFI girls; little 'Chug' Steele, who did a comedy parson routine; Eric Hayes, a fiddle player with a wicked sense of humour who, because of his gold tooth, was known as the 'flash in the pan'; and Jack Bridgeman from Somerset, who played the clarinet, tap danced and also did comedy.

Jack, Eric and Bill Hall would come back pie-eyed from a session in the sergeants' mess and, lying on their backs, would produce sensational music until the guard on picket duty would bang on the side of the tent around dawn to ask for a bit of peace and quiet.

The shows were produced by John Langston, who also played the straight characters when required. Laurie Taylor was a solo pianist who left RATD during the time I was there. We also had a singer from Sheffield whose name was Harold McGee. His speaking voice was quite high, not unlike George Formby's, but when he sang he had the depth and power of an operatic bass. It produced quite a startling effect when he came on to announce in his high-pitched soprano that he was going to sing 'Old Man River', but the titters would stop as soon as he let fly à la Paul Robeson.

To all intents and purposes we were a completely professional company, and when the ENSA parties came to perform in our theatre they were always surprised by the smart dressing-rooms and the lighting boards which Les Dodds had installed. We, in turn, would sit out front and smugly criticize the real professionals, not knowing how much we still had to learn. There is the world of difference between the best amateur and even a mediocre professional comedian, and to cross the gap is an arduous and painful business. But I suppose, considering the circumstances, we could be allowed our little vanities.

I played the Tom Walls part in the Ben Travers farce, *Tons Of Money*, working in a lot of funny business with a false beard, something to which a professional actor would never have resorted, but I must say it used to bring the house down every night.

When VE Day came on 8 May 1945, there was no longer a need for a Royal Artillery Training Depot because we were not going to be firing the big guns any more – not in Europe, anyway. It was decided that because the show was so good, we ought to take it on tour as a kind of travelling fun-fair which, as well as helping to keep all the servicemen happy while they waited to be demobbed, could also be a source of income for the Royal Artillery Fund.

It was a great idea, and we were soon travelling around Italy wherever there were large concentrations of troops, setting up a marquee as our theatre. The fun-fair part of the unit consisted of various games of chance operated by sergeants or warrant officers. One of these was a large wheel of fortune upon which a big metal arrow was fixed. The wheel was divided into segments, like the spokes on a cart-wheel, which were numbered from one to twenty. The punters would place their money on a flat wooden board, similarly numbered, and when the arrow stopped at a particular digit – for example, ten – the winner would receive ten times the amount of lire he had placed on the board, plus his original stake.

There was a sergeant friend of mine who used to take his turn at managing this stall, and whenever I was short of money I would go along to it and try to catch his eye. He would then wink at me and I'd place my lire on twelve or fourteen, and by some strange coincidence my number would always come up. I didn't know how he did it – and I didn't want to know – but I was careful not to try it too often.

At one time a few of us were at a loose end for a few days in Salerno, and having exhausted all the sights and delights of that battered city, we hired a rowing boat and rowed all the way up the coast to the beautiful resort of Amalfi. We liked it so much, that after rowing the boat back to Salerno, Jack Bridgeman, Bill Hall, Eric Hayes and Sammy Lambert packed their instruments and we managed to persuade one of the fun-fair truck drivers to take us all back there.

For two days we lived like lords. The Cappuccini Hotel just outside Amalfi had been taken over as a rest camp for officers, and just a hundred yards or so away, the Santa Catarina had been designated as a warrant officers- and sergeants-only hotel.

Both places were starved of entertainment, and we performed impromptu cabarets there, with Tony Thompson in his element on the Bechstein which the officers' hotel boasted. We were fêted and fed, and it was here in Amalfi that I began trying out a song or two. Previously I had sung only as a joke, doing the Nelson Eddy and Jeanette MacDonald duet, but loosened by a few glasses of vino rosso I belted out a ballad or two, adding my raspberry every time I became embarrassed. It was not until after I started broadcasting that I began to think about adding a song to my routine of impressions.

At the end of the summer of 1945 recruiting began for a new Entertainment Unit to be called the Central Pool of Artists, and as the RATD show was about to break up, Bill Hall and I applied to join. We were both accepted and in due course reported to a building in Vomero, near Naples, which had been taken over as the CPA Headquarters. Here, under the command of Lieutenant-Colonel Phillip Slessor, all the best available talent among the servicemen in Italy was to be gathered in. From this pool of artists, shows were to be put together, rehearsed and sent out on the road all over Italy and the central Mediterranean.

The living quarters were not great, but we all had individual beds, not double bunks, and I sat gratefully on mine as I looked around the room. Bill Hall had dumped his kit all over the floor, as was his wont. He opened his violin case, took out a stale sandwich from some previous officers' mess party and chewed it solemnly. A sad-looking soldier from a recce regiment busied himself with the unloading of his double bass, and a bombardier removed a guitar from its battered case then strummed a few chords. Bill Hall, brushing crumbs off his violin, put it under his chin, his lank hair, which fell either side of his face, making him look for all the world like Paganini. As he started to play along with the guitar, the sad soldier joined in on his double bass. The effect was truly magical, and the rest of us in the room – all new to each other – applauded in sheer delight as Bill Hall, Johnny Mulgrew and Spike Milligan began a musical partnership which was to last for a long time.

Johnny Mulgrew was a dead ringer for Buster Keaton and his sad, deadpan face belied his sly humour. Like Bill Hall, he had been a professional musician, and had once played with the famous Ambrose orchestra. Spike, Johnny and I became friends straight away and I was delighted when it was decided that we were all going to be in a brand new production called *Over the Page*. I was to be the comic, working through the show in sketches as well as doing my own act, and the three lads were to be called the Bill Hall Trio with the star spot – just before the finale.

I didn't know what to make of Spike at first, but when I discovered that it was he who had come looking for the 7.2

gun howitzer back in North Africa, we soon found that we had a lot in common. Then, as now, he was bursting with ideas for way-out comedy sketches, and we shared a dislike for comics who just told jokes. I was also aware that he had experienced a bad time in action and had just been discharged from a psychiatric hospital near Sorrento. There but for the grace of God I too might have gone.

Soon the unit began to fill up as fresh talent came in from all over Italy. Ken Platt (who became well-known for his catch-phrase 'I'll not take my coat off – I'm not stopping') joined us, along with various singers and straight actors who were only too eager to lay down their weapons and start getting back into shape for Civvy Street.

Those performers who were still 'on probation' were tried out at the officers' club which was on the premises. I remember one North Country comic who joined us, sitting on the bed he'd been allotted, feeling the springs and saying gleefully, 'Ain't it grand to be a bloody turn?'

That night he did his audition at the club under the critical gaze of the officers and their lady friends. He opened his act by vamping a few chords on the piano and then, lifting his backside off the piano stool, he broke wind with a pane-rattling ferocity. 'Ain't I a dirty bastard?' he said, grinning at the shocked audience. I'm afraid we never saw the rest of his act, but I'm glad to say he was kept on at CPA in the cookhouse because we all secretly admired his nerve.

One afternoon during rehearsals for *Over the Page* I was detailed to do my act at a hospital concert. The fellow on before me was new to the unit, and when I saw him perform I regretted the fact that I had to follow him. He was a thin young lad who told crazy gags and finished with a very accomplished tap dance, and it was clear that he was no amateur.

After I had finished my turn he came up and congratulated me. 'Are you a pro, then?' he asked.

I was flattered beyond measure, but shook my head. 'I hope to be,' I said. 'Do you think I've got a chance?'

'Of course,' said Norman Vaughan, and became my friend for life.

The run-up to the opening night of *Over the Page* became frantic with fittings for costumes and rehearsals for sketches and dance routines. They had me leaping around in a ballet scene with three other blokes and four Italian girls, who were about as flat-footed as I was. We were put through our paces by an ex-ballet dancer, Jean Veidt, who used to shed tears at our incompetence.

All this hard work made us very keen to get away for a drink in the evenings and Norman, Spike, Johnny Mulgrew and I used to belt down the stairs from our living quarters as soon as we had changed out of our rehearsal kit. One evening I was a bit late, having decided to dress up my uniform with a fancy scarf under the collar of my battledress blouse, and in my hurry to catch up with the other three I hurtled down the steps straight into Lieutenant-Colonel Slessor, our Commanding Officer. When he'd recovered his breath, he took one look at me and yelled, 'Take that bloody scarf off!'

A few years later, when he was the BBC compère for the radio show *Variety Bandbox*, he announced me as 'my old war-time comrade'. The only words he had ever addressed to me had concerned my scarf. But that's show business, folks!

Spike rather fancied himself as a vocalist and was given a song to sing in, of all things, a gypsy camp-fire scene. He wore a spotted red bandana on his head, perilously close to his eyebrows, and a loose-fitting blouse. His trousers were of hessian material dyed black, and on his feet he wore army plimsolls. A more unlikely gypsy you couldn't imagine as he sang, with feeling, 'Down in the forest, playing his old guitar, lives an old "dreams" man', accompanied by his own guitar. He gets a bit upset whenever I remind him of this episode.

The over-all direction of the show was in the hands of Major Hector Ross, an actor who had frequently played in West End productions and who fortunately thought I was very funny. He had chosen an Italian film star, Luisa Poselli, as the centrepiece of the show, and it was decided that we would open at the Argentina Theatre in Rome.

Special scenery was built in the form of a huge open book, and the idea was that an acrobat dressed as a clown should come on to turn a page at a time, revealing the name of the next act or sketch. Unfortunately, on the opening night the acrobat fractured his ankle and the idea was abandoned.

The orchestra was completely professional and consisted of army and civilian musicians, some of them Jewish refugees.

Altogether it was a well-mounted production, and the opening night was a big success, marred only by the news that Hector Ross was in danger of being court-martialled for exceeding his budget! The hit of the show was undoubtedly the Bill Hall Trio, but I managed to impress the theatre critic for *The Union Jack* newspaper, a Canadian Captain in the British Army by the name of Andy Grey. He came to see me after the show and promised to help me get started after I'd been demobbed.

When we had finished at the Argentina we went to the Bellini Theatre in Naples where Captain William Chappell, the choreographer and revue producer, dropped in to see the show and afterwards told me that the next time he'd see me would be in the West End. Ten years later, when I was topping the bill at the London Palladium, I was told by the stage door-keeper, George Cooper, that a Billy Chappell wanted to speak to me.

'Send him in,' I said, and as Billy walked into the dressing-room I asked him, 'Where have you been till now?'

The tour took in Florence, Milan, Bologna and other big cities, and Spike and I chased girls, discussed philosophy, but most of all wondered what would become of us when were demobbed. That time was getting nearer for me. Owing to the fact that I had been in the army as a Territorial since April 1939, I had quite a bit of service under my belt, and it was length of service and age which determined what number demobilization group a soldier was given. Although I was still only twenty-five years of age, I was designated Group 28.

When you knew what number you were, the agonizing wait began for the news that your group was due to be called.

Over the Page closed eventually and I found myself hanging about in Naples again. Ivor Williams had turned up at CPA and was making himself useful as a stage-manager. I was glad to see him, because I didn't know anyone else there. Norman was out on tour in another show and I applied for permission to join him. Meanwhile, Ivor and I frequented the local bars and cafés. One night I sat at a table and recorded my impressions of my surroundings. I still have the piece of paper, and because it was a first-hand account of a long-vanished moment in time, here it is in its entirety. It's called 'Italian Café'.

'Band of quarrelling musicians. Three waitresses – one fat, one tall and thin, one deformed but pretty. Little girl with

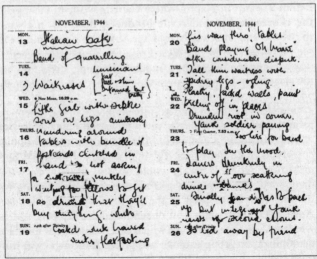

septic sores on legs, aimlessly wandering around tables with bundle of postcards clutched in hand – not asking for customers, mutely waiting for fellows to get so drunk what they'd buy anything. White-coated, white-haired waiter flat-footing his way thro' tables. Band playing 'Oy Maria' after considerable dispute. Tall, thin waitress with spidery legs – ogling. Flashy faded walls, paint peeling off in places. Drunken riot in corner. Yank soldier paying 500 lire for band to play 'In The Mood'. Dances drunkenly in centre of floor, scattering drinks and drunks. Finally band has to pack up but indignant Yank insists on second chorus. Is led away by friend.'

My application to join Norman's show came through and I hitch–hiked my way from Naples all the way up to Mestre – just outside Venice. The night I arrived I was informed that it was the final performance – the show was coming off. I insisted on doing my act, on principle, and the following day we set off back for Naples. Norman and I happened to be on a truck that conveniently broke down in Rome, and we spent a quite hysterical few days in a hotel near the Central Station called the Albergo Universo. It was a rather drunken spree, until one afternoon we went to a cinema and saw *The Lost Weekend*. The film made tee-totallers of both of us for at least two days.

When we did eventually get back to base at Vomero I found that my group number was now due for demobilization and after saying my farewells and exchanging addresses with Norman and Ivor I set off for the demob centre, Lammie Camp. It was a tented base camp on the side of Mount Vesuvius which was almost ankle-deep in lava dust from a recent eruption. I spent a couple of anxious days here waiting for my name to appear on the lists posted outside the camp office. There was no one I knew there and I missed the company of my old friends. Spike had decided to get demobbed in Italy and remained with CPA as a civilian. The Bill Hall Trio was in great demand, and he thought he'd stay with it for a while.

It was a strange time for me. I had been in the army for seven years and had been dying to get out of it. And yet, faced now with the prospect of leaving and making my own way in the world, I felt very insecure. Home, of course, was beckoning and I was really looking forward to seeing the family again. I had been home for four weeks in August 1945 and had had a great time, but I could not see myself settling down in Swansea after I'd seen so much of the world and had a taste of the theatre. I had plenty to think about on the long train and boat journey back to Aldershot.

CHAPTER SEVEN

Out of the Frying Pan into the Foyer

I had first come to Aldershot in December 1940 as Gunner Secombe, H D 924378, and now, in April 1946, I was leaving it as Mr Harry Secombe, in a pin-striped demob suit, new squeaky shoes, a pork-pie hat and a light blue overcoat. In a pocket nestled a Post Office savings bank book containing £82 gratuity and a one-way travel warrant back to Swansea.

The family gave me a tremendous welcome when I got home, making admiring remarks about my tan and on how long and bleached my hair had become. In spite of Spike's description of me at about this time in one of his books as a fat, sweaty idiot, I was in fact fairly slim, weighing under twelve stone. My mother, like all mothers, was sure that I hadn't been eating properly and began to make huge meals for me in the first few days I was home.

Home was now at 48 Hazel Road in Uplands, Swansea. The folks had been bombed in Grenfell Park Road whither we had moved, just before the war, from the house in St Leger Crescent – a short trip of about one hundred yards for the removal van. The Uplands was quite a posh area, very close to where Dylan Thomas lived. But I have to admit that I never even saw him. Mind you, I don't think he ever saw me, either.

My homecoming was a joyous reunion with Carol and Fred and all my relatives, but my attempts to tell them about the fighting I had seen were countered by their tales of the bombings that Swansea and its surrounding district had suffered. I couldn't get a word in edgeways – but it was great to be home.

A couple of days after I'd been demobbed I met some of the lads from the regiment in a pub in town and we arranged to go to a dance the following night. I had no regular girl-friend – the only girl I had taken out was called Elsie Rew, but she had eventually deserted me for a taller suitor before I went overseas.

And so Danny Williams, Josh Jones, Vic Kelly, myself and a few other mates from 132 Field Regiment met at the Mumbles Pier Dance Hall, a few miles out of town on the electric railway. It was packed that night, and after a few beers I plucked up enough courage to ask a pretty, dark-eyed girl for a dance. I took off my glasses out of sheer vanity and sauntered over to where she stood chatting with a couple of her friends. I was going through my 'Canadian phase' at the time, the result of playing a lumberjack in a sketch, and I also happened to be wearing the heavy red-and-black checked shirt I had removed from the property basket before I left *Over the Page*.

'Can I have this dance, please?' I pretended to chew gum as I spoke.

'Pardon?' said the girl.

I repeated my request, toning down the fake accent a bit, and swept my four-foot eleven-inch partner on to the dance floor. Forty-four years later we're still dancing – not quite so nimbly perhaps, but Myra can still do a pretty good 'fish tail'.

She had been about to leave for her home in Pennard where she lived with her parents in a holiday bungalow, their house in Manselton having been destroyed in the blitz, but one of her friends persuaded her to stay at her place in Swansea for the night. I saw Myra to the Mumbles train, escorted by a phalanx of her pals, and made arrangements to meet her the following night outside the Plaza Cinema at six o'clock.

The next morning I had quite a hangover, and for the life of me I couldn't remember what my date for the evening looked like. I decided that I would arrive early at the Plaza, get behind one of the pillars outside the cinema and keep a furtive watch. If I didn't fancy what I saw I'd stay where I was and forget the whole thing. It was at a quarter past six when, tired of waiting, I stepped out from behind my pillar to go home, just as Myra daintily made an appearance from behind hers. And in this atmosphere of mutual mistrust, our courtship began.

It was a glorious summer that year, and Myra and I spent a lot of time together. We used to go down to the many beautiful beaches on the Gower coast and laze on the sand, or go for long walks along the gorse-clad cliffs. We fed lamb sandwiches to sheep in Pwlldu, and I sprained my arm trying to make pebbles skip on the sea at Pobbles Bay. In the evening we'd go to the pictures and once a week we'd pay a visit to the Swansea Empire. Every time I saw a show there I'd be filled

---

RICHARD THOMAS & BALDWINS LIMITED

Memorandum from	*To* Mr. Seccombe,
COLLIERIES SECTION :—	Hazel Road,
41, WIND STREET,	Uplands,
SWANSEA.	SWANSEA.
Dept.	*Your Ref.*
	Our Ref. FEJ/WT. Date 29th July 1946.

Dear Sir,

      I wish to contact your son Harry, who was formerly employed at this office, and I should be obliged if you would forward me his present address. I may say that I have some information to his advantage which I wish to convey to him.

           Yours faithfully,
      FOR RICHARD THOMAS & BALDWINS LIMITED.

          (COLLIERIES SECTION)

with the desire to get up on the stage myself and show them what I could do.

It was time that I did just that, and after having politely refused an offer of my old job back at Baldwins – they were a very forgiving firm – I wrote to Andy Grey as I had promised. He was the Canadian Captain who had offered to help me after seeing my act in *Over the Page* in Rome.

I went up to London to meet him and he suggested that I applied to the Windmill Theatre for an audition. This was the theatre which featured nudes and comedians in a revue which ran for six shows a day, six days a week – a total of thirty-six performances a week. It was a gruelling schedule, especially for the comedians who had to battle to get the attention of an audience which had only come in to see the nudes. Men in dirty raincoats would fight to get a seat in the front row of the tiny theatre, while on stage some unfortunate comic would be trying to get laughs. However, it was a marvellous show-case for any performer due to its situation in the West End, just off Shaftesbury Avenue, and it really was a matter of 'if you can get a laugh here – you'll get a laugh anywhere'.

To my delight, mixed with trepidation, I received a letter from the Windmill management offering me an audition.

I went up to London on the train the day before the audition and stayed the night in Ilford with my cousin Margaret – Uncle Harry's daughter from Llangyfelach – who was sharing a house with a fellow teacher, Joan Fox. They gave me a good meal that night and sent me on my way, wishing me all the luck in the world and waving crossed fingers as I got on the bus for the West End early the next morning.

The audition was not until 9.30 am, and at 8 o'clock I was wandering around Piccadilly in a muck sweat of fear and apprehension. All around were hoardings featuring star names advertising the latest shows, and I felt very inadequate. In the battered attaché case I carried, my shaving mug rattled in sympathy with my knees as I surveyed the huge board outside the Windmill which listed the names of all the famous

Our wedding day, 19 February 1948: (*left to right*) Beryl Atherton (Myra's cousin), Josh Williams (best man, later to marry Carol), Jim Atherton (Myra's father) and sister Carol.

With Norman Vaughan (*left to right*), Johnny Mulgrew and Myra in London, 1948.

Returning from a rough fishing trip in Brixham harbour, 1949, with father-in-law, Jim.

With my mother, Gladys.

Proud grandparents.

Above: Baby minding is a serious business, Torquay, 1949.

Right: Jennifer, asleep at last, on the front at Rhyl.

Jennifer with Myra, my
mother, Carol and neighbour.

Jennifer, age 2.

With Jennifer in 1950.

In yellow bowler
hat and check
jacket for the
'Toot, toot tootsie'
number in the
Blackpool season
of 1951 – a
lovely mover.

At the opening of
St Stephen's Garden
Party, Blackpool,
1951 – cue for
a song?

Judging a beauty competition with Jack Radcliffe,
Blackpool, 1951. I won.

With fellow artistes backstage in Blackpool: Vera Lynn,
Jack Radcliffe (*at the rear*) and Norman Evans.

With Milligan upstairs at Grafton's – the monkey was the real brains behind the show.

Goons at Grafton's – we could only afford two scripts.

Funny faces on radio.

Persuading the Goons to sign their second contract at the
Aeolian Hall, 1951 (*front, left to right*): Dennis Main Wilson,
Jimmy Grafton, Spike Milligan and Larry Stevens. Behind, next
to me, are Michael Bentine and Peter Sellers. The money was
obviously laughable.

In descending order: Michael, Spike, Peter and guess who?

comedians who had appeared there, alongside the year they had made their debuts. Little did I think that one day my name would be up there as the star of 1946.

When I eventually plucked up enough courage to enter the stage door in Archer Street, the backstage area was busy with fellow auditioners preparing for their acts. I asked the stage-manager, a portly chap called Johnny Gale, if I could possibly have a small table. He gave me a grin. 'All right, mate, take that gold one over there.' He pointed to a rather delicate-looking piece of furniture in a corner of the prop room. I thanked him and proceeded to prepare it for my act. First of all I laid some newspaper on it, and then, having filled my mug with water from a basin in the toilet, I began to get lathered up.

Johnny Gale saw me and tapped me on the shoulder. 'You should have done that before you came here, lad,' he said gruffly.

I turned to him, my face full of Yardley's shaving soap. 'It's my act,' I said.

He clapped a hand to his forehead. 'Gawd Almighty,' he said, moving quickly away.

I had already given my sheet of music to a sympathetic Ronnie Bridges, who was one of the two regular accompanists at the theatre, and told him roughly what I wanted. He made a couple of helpful suggestions, and I felt a little less nervous as I stood in the wings, constantly lathering away as I waited my turn.

One of the acts on in front of me was a short, stocky lad who was also ex-army. We wished each other luck and I watched as he went on to do his audition. He told one joke, fell down, and before he could rise to his feet, a voice from the blackness of the auditorium said, 'Thank you, that will be all.' It was Vivian Van Damm, the famous impresario who ran the Windmill, who was sitting out front along with his producer, Ann Mitelle. Norman Wisdom left the stage door shortly afterwards to make a fortune.

The act immediately before me was a Chinese illusionist whose elaborate make-up and carefully organized props suggested that he must have been up all night getting ready. He went on, shuffled forward in Chinese style, and bowed.

'Thank you,' said the voice of Van Damm, and the stunned illusionist was dismissed before he'd even done a trick.

Before I could take in his demise, I heard my name called. Ronnie Bridges swung into a chorus of 'Wild About Harry' and I was on stage, pierced by the spotlight and wondering what time the next train to Swansea left Paddington. I launched myself into the well-tried routine, scattering lather all over the stage, expecting that at any minute the voice out front would call, 'Thank you – next.' But it didn't come, and I even fancied that I heard faint laughter from the stalls as the act proceeded. When I had finished on the last note of 'Sweethearts', I stood, soap-stained and fearful, waiting for the verdict.

'Come and see me afterwards,' said the voice, and as I gathered up my table and shaving gear I was not sure whether I had got a job or whether I was going to be given a damned good telling-off for wasting the great man's time.

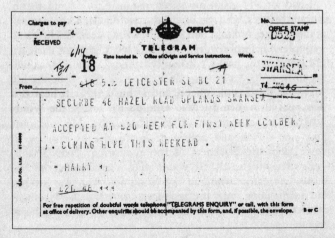

As it transpired, however, I had passed the audition and I was summoned to Ann Mitelle's office to work out the details of my engagement. Ann was a nice, jolly person who told me she and Van Damm liked my act, and asked how much money I was expecting.

I had no idea what to ask. In my mind I could hear the words of Norman Vaughan in one of our many conversations about the business. 'Always ask as high a figure as you can think of and you can always come down.'

A suitably high figure came into my head. I'd been getting three shillings and sixpence a day in the army, and using that as a starting price I said, 'Twenty pounds a week.'

'Done,' said Ann, and I signed a contract there and then for *Revuedeville 187* to begin on 17 October, an auspicious day because it was also my sister Carol's birthday.

I left the theatre with a chorus of angels ringing in my ears, and the first thing I did was to send two telegrams home, one to Mam and one to Myra to tell them the good news. 'Have been accepted at Windmill at twenty pounds a week' was the substance of the first one, and I pushed the form under the grille to the girl behind the counter expecting at least an eyebrow raised in admiration. She counted the words expressionlessly and asked me for four shillings. The chorus of angels dimmed and I was back down to earth again.

My gratuity from the army was looking pretty sick by the time I got back from London, so I signed on at the Swansea Labour Exchange as an actor. I used to be the life and soul of the dole queue, and I think the staff heaved a sigh of relief when I left to take up my job at the Windmill.

Myra and I had an 'understanding' by this time and we had both been looked over by our respective parents. My folks thought she was right for me and she passed the 'Uncle Harry test' with flying colours. She sat next to him at tea-time at our house and was on her best behaviour. Uncle Harry was not. When peaches and cream were served, he said to Myra, 'Do you like those?'

'Yes, thank you,' she said.

'I'm glad,' said my wicked Uncle Harry, 'because I've just dropped my glass eye in your dish.'

Myra didn't turn a hair. 'If I see something staring back at me,' she said, 'I'll let you know.'

My first encounter with Myra's relatives was when I was taken to meet her Uncle Walter and Aunty Elsie in Manselton. I behaved myself, for once, because Myra was very anxious that I should make a good impression. Apparently everything went well and I was over the first domestic hurdle.

However, her grandmother was not very pleased when she found out that Myra's new boyfriend was on the stage. 'Don't bring any actors home here,' was her reaction to the news. So I had to pass the 'Gran test' before I was accepted, but fortunately no glass eyes were involved. I got on well with Myra's parents, Jim and Flo Atherton, and once the initial examinations were over we all enjoyed each others' company.

Before I began work at the Windmill, Andy Grey – who wrote the show business column in the *Weekly Sporting Review* under the name of Ken Gordon – arranged for me to be the cabaret at a party thrown by the publication. I was very nervous before going on, but once I was in the spotlight I felt at home, and the reaction was very warm. This was my first paid engagement, and I was enormously relieved when it was all over. If I could get laughs from people who had paid to see me – and civilians at that – then perhaps I might do well in my new profession. Isador Green, the *Sporting Review*'s editor and founder, had also been in Italy on *The Union Jack*, and promised to give me plenty of free publicity in his paper. He was true to his word, and he and Andy Grey gave me great encouragement in those early days when I was very unsure of myself.

I had fixed up digs in Kilburn for the run of the Windmill Show, at 4 Brondesbury Villas, to be exact. It was a guest house on three floors run by a Mrs Isaacs, a lady who suffered from asthma and, ultimately, me. I began life there as a privileged lodger with a nice room on the first floor, but as my career fluctuated I was moved further up the house, until at one period – after being out of work for several weeks – I found myself sleeping in a converted broom cupboard with my feet quite close to the wash basin. Mrs Isaacs was a nice old lady, and was always concerned that I had enough to eat at breakfast, because that was the only meal of the day to which I was entitled. She had a large marmalade cat which was always sitting in the dining-room when I came down just before breakfast was about to be cleared away. Usually by this time the other lodgers had gone off to work and I was left to finish what remained on the table. This sometimes involved me in a fight with the cat for the last kipper. The damned thing never liked me and would take every opportunity to give me a side swipe with its claws. I hated the animal.

That first week at the Windmill I was so determined to make an impression on my first appearance that I gave my 'all', forgetting that there were five more shows to do that day.

Jimmy Edwards was the resident comedian at the time and he gave me some good advice: 'Pace yourself, mate – there are ninety–nine steps up to the dressing-room and you've got to climb them at least seven times a day.'

He didn't seem to have any nerves at all. Perhaps after what he'd been through as a pilot at Arnhem, the Windmill seemed like a picnic. He had won the DFC for landing his Dakota plane after being hit by anti-aircraft fire, refusing to bale out and leave his crew behind. I admired him tremendously, especially when I watched his act from the wings. He used to sit on a beer crate in his dressing-gown pretending to read bits of a newspaper to the audience. When they started to clamber over the front row to get to the best seats he used to insult them, and they loved him for it.

The leading dancer, Keith Lester, certainly didn't love me for leaving the stage full of water and soap suds, and he complained bitterly to Johnny Gale. It must have been very difficult to follow my act with a dance routine, because apart from anything else, the floor of the tiny stage was made of glass. We reached a compromise eventually and I did a couple of gags in front of the curtain while the stage-hands mopped up the mess I'd made.

Someone else who had reservations about my performance was Vivian Van Damm, who was known to one and all as V D. He was coming down the stairs from the dressing-rooms one day during my first week, and he met me as I was half-way up after coming off stage from my second performance of the day.

'Secombe,' he said. 'That noise you make with your mouth . . .' He attempted a raspberry and failed miserably.

'You mean this?' I blew one of my best efforts for the boss.

'Yes, that,' he said. I waited proudly for acclamation. 'Cut it out,' said V D, 'I don't like it.' And he continued on his way down the steps.

I was devastated – half my act was gone! For the next couple of days I struggled valiantly to remove the raspberry stain from my performance, but it didn't seem the same, and the audience sensed my unease. Then one day, as I was coming down from the dressing-room on my way to the stage, still worried about the gap in my act, I met VD who, on this ocasion, was on the way up.

'I've been thinking about that noise you make,' he said, without attempting to do it himself.

'This – er – sound?' I blew a half-hearted Bronx cheer.

'That's it,' said VD. 'Put it back in.'

I went on stage for my next performance and filled the theatre with a welter of raspberries.

During my time at the 'Mill' I was besieged with visitors wanting to see me backstage – friends from the army, relatives, and quite a lot of curate colleagues of my brother, who was now the Reverend Fred. It was the custom to take anyone who came to see a performer to the canteen for a cup of tea, and it was only after the first week that I realized that I was not the real reason for the backstage visits. The ladies of the chorus would sit around the canteen in their stage costumes with, at the most, a scanty dressing-gown tossed carelessly over their shoulders. All the time I was at the Windmill I don't think any of my visitors ever looked directly at me in the canteen, and I've never seen so many spilled cups of tea, either.

One visitor who came backstage was genuinely only interested in me and my performance. His name was Cecil Madden and he happened to be a BBC television producer. He was always on the look-out for fresh talent for the fledgling medium, and the Windmill had a reputation for putting on new comedians. Thanks to him I was invited to do a spot on a variety show called *Rooftop Rendezvous* which led to quite a few subsequent TV appearances.

Something else happened during my stint at the Windmill that I knew nothing about until the day of Jimmy Edwards's funeral, when I met up again with script-writers Frank Muir and Denis Norden. Frank, who had known Jimmy in the RAF, had recommended him as a potential comedian for a new series that a BBC radio producer was about to launch. Consequently the producer sent a colleague along to the Windmill to have a look at Jimmy's act.

He came back from seeing the show and reported to the producer that he didn't think Edwards was any good. 'Waste of time,' he said. 'He comes on and does a bloody awful piece of business with a shaving brush and blows raspberries all the time. He won't get anywhere.' So Jim didn't get the job.

Towards the end of the six-week run of the show I began to get rather weary and my face was starting to feel the effect of being shaved seven times a day – though only once with a blade in the razor. I remember waiting for a bus back to Kilburn one Saturday night when a light drizzle began. By the time the bus arrived some ten minutes later, soap bubbles were forming in my hair and the West Indian conductor took a step back from me as I mounted the platform. 'Ju-ju!' he cried, crossing himself. I was too tired even to raise a raspberry.

There was one place in Great Windmill Street to which everybody in the show's company seemed to gravitate – Allen's Club, it was called, and it was run by Daddy Allen and his wife. We all called him 'Daddy', but nobody ever told me why. It was a small drinking-club with a little restaurant attached, and a lot of us went there because Daddy Allen ran a slate. This meant that we could eat on 'tick', paying our bills when we got our wages. The club was in a very convenient position, just across the way from the Windmill stage door, and it was easy to slip a coat on and nip over for a drink or a meal between performances. When Myra came to town to see me, the poor girl saw nothing at all of the bright lights of the West End – just the inside of Daddy Allen's Club.

It was a rendezvous for a whole posse of up-and-coming comedians. Frank Muir would meet up with Jimmy Edwards there; Alfred Marks was a frequent visitor, and so was Bill Kerr, the Australian comic who has since turned into such a fine straight actor. When Norman Vaughan was demobbed he used to meet me there, and I remained a member for many years. Someone else who frequented the club was Michael Bentine.

I first saw Mike at the dress rehearsal for the show that followed the one in which I had made my debut at the Windmill. He and a pianist named Tony Sherwood performed a crazy double act called Sherwood and Forrest – Mike being 'Forrest'. Their performance consisted of a wild musical act all done in 'cod' Russian, with Tony on piano and Mike playing drums. My sides ached from laughing at their antics, and I went backstage and introduced myself to them. Mike had already seen my shaving routine and congratulated me on my fresh approach to comedy. The two of us got on like wildfire and we were to spend many hysterical hours in Lyon's Corner House which, in those days, was open all night. We'd stay there till dawn talking about the things we'd like to do in the theatre.

He was a slim, curly-haired lad then, full of restless energy and throwing out ideas for comedy situations like sparks from a Catherine wheel. During the war he had been in the RAF and had finished up in Intelligence, a fact which impressed me no end. I was still mentally a lance-bombardier and I felt sometimes a little inferior to all these ex-officers I was mixing with. One of them was Reg O'List, who had been a major with CPA in Italy, and whom I had often had to salute. Now he was a singer and guitarist at the Windmill, where he'd worked before being called up. He was delighted that I was now a fully-fledged performer and even gave me one of his suits. I accepted it with enthusiasm – my demob suit was getting to look a little threadbare, and the money I was earning after I had finished my engagement at the 'Mill' was practically non-existent.

I managed to get a broadcast on the Carroll Levis show as a 'star from the services', thanks to the good offices of Levis himself, who kept his promise to me back in Bari. When the *Radio Times* appeared for that week I couldn't wait to open it and see my name in print. I turned the pages with trembling hands. There it was . . . 'Harry Fecombe, a successful discovery,' it said. This was the first of many occasions on which my name was misspelt. I was to be called everything from Seagrave to Snelgrove, and later, when my agent decided I should have some kind of descriptive title on the programmes, I became 'the golden-voiced Goon', which usually finished up as 'the golden-voiced Coon'.

For the Carroll Levis programme I received ten guineas which didn't last all that long, and apart from the odd cabaret date I managed to wangle through the influence of Andy Grey, there was not much work for me in the final weeks of 1946.

It was a time when the business was becoming swamped with returning ex-servicemen who had had a taste of performing in army or RAF concert parties and were now, like myself, eager to try their luck in show business. People like Benny Hill, Tommy Cooper, Frankie Howerd, Max Bygraves, Norman Wisdom, Dick Emery, Eric Sykes, Peter Sellers, Arthur English – all different from each other in style, and all clamouring for a chance to show what they could do.

I remember once sitting in the BBC canteen in the basement of the Aeolian Hall Studios in Bond Street. A lot of comics would go down there for a cheap, subsidized meal on the pretext of meeting some non-existent producer. A chap came and sat opposite me and, over a cup of tea, Max Bygraves announced that he was thinking of packing it in. 'I could go back to carpentering,' he told me. 'I've still got my tools.'

'You're lucky,' I said. 'I can't do anything – I haven't got a proper trade.'

CHAPTER EIGHT

Learning the Trade

Christmas 1946 was spent at home. Back at my digs in Brondesbury Villas, Kilburn, I was now in the converted broom cupboard, and poor Mrs Isaacs was having to wait for the rent. The euphoria of playing the Windmill Theatre and being a 'rising comedy star' had worn off and it was difficult meeting old army friends in the dole queue. They all thought that I had hit the big time. Myra, of course, was glad to see my face again, as were Mam and Dad, but I was desperate to get more work.

Then I had a bit of luck. I was offered a tour of Germany with a Combined Services Entertainment Show featuring Peter Waring, a popular radio comedian, and Adelaide Hall, the coloured singer. Sam Kydd, Pamela Matthews, Pamela Cundell, Harry Robins, the xylophone player, a dance troupe and myself were among the supporting cast.

We went out to Germany in January, sailing from Hull in bitterly cold weather. When we got to Hamburg there was thick snow everywhere and one night at the Garrison Theatre, the water actually froze in my shaving mug before I went on. Everywhere there was devastation and people were dropping dead in the streets from hunger and exposure.

The star of the show, Peter Waring, was a strange character who claimed to have been a Lieutenant-Commander in the Royal Navy, but eventually turned out to have served as a fireman in the London Fire Brigade. He was an excellent raconteur who was always immaculately dressed in white tie and tails. The man responsible for keeping his suits pressed and seeing that his shirts were blindingly white was a lad called Bill Montague who was always darkly suspicious of his boss's claim to have been in the Royal Navy, but could never prove it. He and I, along with Sam Kydd, used to make the most of what was a rather arduous trip. Sam had been a prisoner of war and had a lot of reasons to be glad to see the Germans suffer, but the deprivation that we saw all around us as we travelled through the shattered cities of the Ruhr and into Berlin, affected him as much as it did the rest of us.

Poor old Peter Waring had a sad end not too long after we got back from Germany. He hanged himself in a cell where he was being held on a fraud charge. I always felt sorry for him because he was obviously playing a part all the time he was off stage, and could never afford to relax in case he gave himself away. And yet we were all prepared to accept him for what he really was – a remarkably good comedian who was possibly the best story-teller (apart from Terry-Thomas) that I have ever come across.

The money I received for the tour allowed me to buy an engagement ring for Myra. She had seen one for forty pounds in a jeweller's window in Swansea, and that was the one I presented her with shortly after I got back from Germany.

In May I had another television engagement on a variety show and the next month I passed an audition for 'Variety Bandbox'. This was the really big radio comedy show of the time, with people like Frankie Howerd and Derek Roy alternating as resident comedians. The producer was Joy Russell-Smith who was very good at spotting new talent, and had given many of us new boys a chance to shine. Bill Kerr, who used to begin his very laconic act with the statement, 'I've only got four minutes', was another young act she had been the first to encourage.

I can't remember exactly what I did for my first 'Bandbox', but I know that part of it was a rather wicked take-off of someone doing animal impressions. I finished with the 'Sweet-hearts' duet accompanied on the piano by Ronnie Bridges, the musician who had been so helpful at my Windmill audition. The act was received quite well and, as I have already related, I had a nice introduction from the resident announcer, Phillip Slessor.

Norman Vaughan was now back in Civvy Street and intro-duced me to his agent, who kindly offered me a date at the Grand Theatre, Bolton, where Norman was already booked. It was to be my first music hall – I had played quite a lot of night-clubs in the sleazier parts of Soho and dark, somewhat dangerous venues like the Blue Lagoon and the Panama Club, where the clientèle was as shady as the wallpaper. This, then, was my chance to break into the more profitable and slightly more respectable area of the variety theatre.

Norman fixed digs for us in the town and we met there on the Sunday night. I was staying down in Swansea with my folks by then, having abandoned my pied à terre in Kilburn, where even the broom cupboard had become too expensive for my slender resources.

'We'll have to get along to the band call early,' said Norman over breakfast. 'The first acts to get their band parts down on the stage have their rehearsal with the orchestra before anybody else, regardless of how far down the bill they are. It's first come, first served.'

I was learning all the time, suddenly realizing how little I knew about the proper theatre.

'What do you work in?' asked the stage-manager after we'd put our music in position, Norman's brightly covered orchestrations making my solo piano part look very poor indeed.

'A white shirt and black trousers,' I replied.

Norman grinned. 'No, he means what kind of curtain do you want to work in front of when you do your act? The street cloth, the one with shops and houses painted on it or the ordinary black tabs?'

'What do you think?' I asked.

'Perhaps the blacks,' Norman decided. 'You'd look funny shaving in a street.'

I sat in the stalls while Norman did his rehearsal with the orchestra, marvelling at the way he got exactly what he wanted, giving instructions to the drummer that were completely new to me. 'I'll have the temple blocks there, Charlie,' and 'Give me a "boom-boom" at the end of the lion-tamer gag.'

When my turn came I was petrified. 'Where's the rest of your music, son?' asked the bewildered conductor, waving my single sheet of piano music in the air.

Norman again came to my rescue. 'Give him a few bars of "I'm Just Wild About Harry" to get him on – you can busk that, lads, and then it's just piano for the "Sweethearts" duet, and finish with "Wild About Harry" as a chaser.'

The band leader shrugged his shoulders and raised his stick. 'All right, let's give it a go.' It was a good orchestra and they 'busked' what was to become my signature tune with no difficulty at all. I explained to the pianist what I did with the 'Sweethearts' duet, and my first-ever band call was over in less than four minutes, which pleased the lads in the pit. Norman's meticulous rehearsal had taken a good fifteen minutes and they were already looking at their watches to see how long they had to go before opening time.

The theatre was absolutely packed that night. It was Wakes Week in Bolton and the whole town was on holiday. I stood in the wings lathering for the act and heard roars of laughter coming from the audience as two men dressed in comedy kilts did funny walks and performed miracles on a tightrope. They came off to thunderous applause, and then the lights went down and Norman introduced me on the off-stage mike as 'The star from "Variety Bandbox" ', which is what I had asked him to say.

I came on carrying the table with my shaving mug, brush and razor on it, and a towel slung over my shoulder.

'Hello, folks!' I said, my lips cleaving to my gums in a death's-head grin. 'I've only just arrived in the theatre. The train was late and I haven't had a chance to shave yet. So as I'm doing it, I'll give you some idea of how other people shave . . .' And I went into my usual routine of the small boy shaving with his father's razor.

The audience sat grimly in their seats. 'This lad hasn't had the decency to shave before coming on to entertain us' seemed to be their attitude, and I went through my performance without getting so much as a titter. In my nervousness I actually swallowed some of the soapy water in the mug instead of spitting it out, and my throat was on fire as I struggled to reach the soprano register for the Jeanette MacDonald part of 'Sweethearts'. I finished on a cracked note, bowed, picked up my table and props and walked off stage accompanied only by the sound of my own footsteps.

Norman helped me off with the table. 'Don't worry,' he said. 'They're always tough here on a Monday first house.' I took some comfort from that, but an icy chill seized my heart when I went for a much-needed drink in the interval, heavily disguised, with my overcoat collar turned up. All around me, as I sipped my rum and pep, I could hear the word 'shaving' being bandied about, sometimes in bewilderment, at other times with sheer lynch-mob fervour. When the bell sounded for the interval I ordered another drink and a large man who had his back to me heard the sound of my voice and turned to face me.

'It was you,' he said accusingly. 'You're that shaving feller.'

I nodded, trying to smile and failing.

'You should be ashamed of yourself. You're Welsh, aren't yer? You ought to be down a mine somewhere doing some real work.'

I was stung by this. 'Who do you think you're talking to?' I said. It was not the cleverest remark I've ever made, but it was all that came to mind.

'I know who you are,' he said. 'But do you know who I am?'

I had to admit that I didn't.

'I own this theatre,' he said. And he followed up this shattering news with: 'You can get t'train in t'morning. You'll not shave in my bloody time.'

And that was it – I was paid off, the thing that every comedian dreads.

I had one tiny triumph though. Norman had arranged for a stage-hand to come on in his act. After he had told the audience, 'My father was a lion-tamer. Every day for years he used to put his head in the lion's mouth. Ladies and gentlemen – my father,' he gestured to the wings and on would come the stage-hand wearing a lion-tamer's uniform which buttoned right up over the top of his bonce, making him appear headless.

That night I persuaded Norman to let me do the 'headless lion-tamer', and as I came on from the side of the stage I undid a couple of buttons on the uniform and gave that audience as juicy a raspberry as I've ever blown.

The next day I got on the first train out of town, leaving behind a sympathetic Norman and a week's rent which the landlady insisted that I paid. All the way back to Swansea I reflected on my future, and actually considered going back to Baldwins.

When I arrived home the first thing I did was to send a telegram to Mike Bentine which read, 'Audience with me all the way. Managed to shake them off at the station.'

That was sheer bravado because I was deeply worried about what would happen the following week when I was due to play the Empire, Oldham, which Norman's agent had also booked for me. It was obvious that the news of what had happened at Bolton would have spread around the business like a fire in a paint factory, and there was no way that I could keep it a secret.

I decided that attack was the best method of defence and so I placed an advertisement in *The Stage*, the weekly theatrical newspaper.

It began 'Vide Press' and listed imaginary notices I had received: '". . . and Larry Felcombe"' – *Blackpool Argus*. "Harvey Snelgrove also featured" – *Bradford Examiner*. "Larry Stenchcombe should not have been on the bill" – *Bolton Bugle*. With only one adverse criticism how can this lad fail?'

A lot of the older pros appreciated the fact that I wasn't going to be too daunted by my failure. Two of them were topping the bill the following week at the Empire, Oldham – Reub Silver and Marian Day, piano duettists who were very popular radio performers. They gave me lots of encouragement that day, helping me through my band call, and they were in the wings to give me moral support as I went on in the second spot – the position on the bill after the dancing girls had done their first routine.

In the prompt corner the stage-manager was all set to give me a 'blackout' and get me off the stage if I was as bad an act as he had been led to believe. But he did not have to pull any switches that night. From the moment I went on, the audience was ready to laugh and my confidence grew with every second. I came off with a good solid round of applause which was echoed in the wings by Reub and Marian, and the fear that had half-strangled me receded in the warm glow of their appreciation.

To this day I cannot fully understand why I could be so disastrously received in Bolton and yet the following week, only a few miles away in Oldham, I was a moderate success. 'That's show business,' as they say, and I don't suppose any of us in the profession can ever predict what's going to happen when we go out to face the public. If we did, everybody would be a star and there would be no supporting acts.

After Oldham I went back to London and began to look for more work with the BBC. It was essential in those days to appear as often as possible on something like 'Variety Band-box' to keep your name before the public. And if you had a catchphrase it was a good handle for them to remember you by.

The ideal way to conduct a career was to make a name on radio and having done so, go out on the Halls to exploit it. The fact that the BBC didn't pay much money was vastly compensated for by the salaries the variety theatres were prepared to hand out to the radio stars. The infant medium, television, was not considered to be much help in making a name because so few people could view it.

The most important item in my new itinerary for success was to find a good scriptwriter. Michael Bentine was very generous with ideas for some of the 'Variety Bandbox' broadcasts I was getting on a semi-regular basis, but he was busy making a career for himself. The problem was solved one lunchtime when Michael took me to a pub he knew in Victoria. It was known as Grafton's and was in Strutton Ground, a turning off Victoria Street. A tall smiling man behind the bar greeted Mike like an old friend, and when I was introduced he laughed. 'Ah – you're the lad from "Variety Bandbox".'

I was flattered that he knew my name and it turned out that he wrote scripts for Derek Roy, one of the resident comedians on the programme, who happened to be his second cousin. We didn't know this at first. It was only after Mike and I had spent about ten minutes criticizing Roy that Jimmy Grafton told us that he wrote his material. He didn't seem to mind the criticism and our visit extended well beyond lunchtime and into the early evening. We discussed every aspect of comedy from the Marx Brothers to the current crop of radio comics. It was a most propitious day for me, because this was the place where 'The Goon Show' was to be born, and in due course Jimmy Grafton was to become my agent and manager. However, at that time, all I knew was that our host had been a Major in the Beds and Herts, had played a vital part in the relief of Arnhem – and was prepared to write scripts for me.

The Bill Hall Trio were now back from working for Combined Services Entertainment and I was able to introduce Mike Bentine to the man I had been raving about – Spike

Milligan. I can't remember exactly where we all met up, but I think it must have been at Grafton's, because that was where I now spent a lot of my time. Jimmy and his wife, Dorothy, were very generous with free meals for starving comics and were even prepared to loan us a couple of quid from the till every so often.

I had now moved into a flat in Linden Gardens, Bayswater, with Norman Vaughan and another bloke called Roy, who was a trumpeter in a band. The place was only supposed to accommodate two people, but we used to take turns to sleep on the floor. Reg O'List and his wife, Jennifer – who were both at the Windmill – also had an apartment in the building, and eventually Spike and Johnny Mulgrew moved into another flat.

We had a lot of fun at Linden Gardens, even though none of us had much money. We were not too well liked by the people who ran the place – we were always slamming the door and making a noise. Once we attempted to make spaghetti in the bath on a gas ring. It turned out to be not only a culinary disaster, but took a lot of enamel off the tub.

There was also the time when I borrowed Spike's Crombie overcoat – we were the same size then, apart from height – because my demob one had become too shabby to wear. I walked about in it for a month, until one day when I was absolutely strapped for cash I sold it to a second-hand clothing dealer for thirty shillings. To my everlasting shame I told him that someone had pinched it in a restaurant, and it was only a few years ago that I could bring myself to tell Spike the truth. He laughed.

There was one venue in the West End of London which always provided a wonderful 'shop window' – and a meal for young ex-services performers. It was called The Nuffield Centre and catered exclusively for servicemen in London. It was run by a lady called Mary Cook who provided coffee and sandwiches in lieu of a fee and was always a great help to aspiring comics. She seemed to know every agent and BBC

producer in London and tipped them off when she thought
a performer showed promise.

The Green Room there was a great meeting place for those
of us she liked – and we were legion. The names of the acts
who were appearing at The Nuffield were published every
week in *The Stage* and in *The Performer*, the trade papers
for the variety profession, and enterprising agents would rub
shoulders with the raw talent on view. Many a big name comic
began his career at The Nuffield and Mary Cook, God bless
her, was like a fairy godmother to us all in those early days
after the war.

Things began to buck up towards the end of 1947 when I
was offered the part of the Dame in the pantomime *Dick
Whittington*, which was to open at the East Ham Palace
and then do a tour of the other venues that were called
'The Syndicate Theatres' – The Empress, Brixton; The Palace, Walthamstow; and The Palace, Chelsea. It was a good
contract and meant that I could start saving up to get married.
The only snag was that I had never before played any part
in a pantomine, except for the Fairy Queen in the RATD
show, and I knew nothing about how to play the Dame,
probably the most traditional role of all. To make matters
worse, I had only ever seen one pantomime in my life. It
was at the Grand Theatre, Swansea, when I was about ten
– and I didn't see much of it, because I was sitting behind
a pillar.

I went along to my first read-through of the script in
the bar of the East Ham Palace, filled with foreboding. I
was introduced to the rest of the cast and sat with the
others on chairs placed in a semi-circle. The principal boy
was Delyse Hendy, a friendly lady whose husband was the
director, Charles King. The principal girl was a tiny lady
called Dot who played the piano accordion, and the leading
comedian was a very funny man by the name of Hal Blue
who was also a very accomplished tap dancer. In addition,

there was a straight actor who was playing Demon Rat, and a quite elderly gentleman in a long back overcoat who was on his hands and knees on the floor. Thinking he had lost something I got down alongside him and offered to help him find the missing item. 'Piss off, I'm Puss,' he said, not unkindly.

As the read-through progressed I became aware that there was not much substance in the part I had to play. Every so often I'd come across notes like 'Dame does business with knitting' or 'This is where Idle Jack and Dame do "I'm not here" gag'. I was completely mystified by this but was afraid to ask what it all meant. However I managed to nod intelligently when Charles King said, 'You know what goes on there,' whenever these bits came up. It also came as a blow when I was told that I had to provide my own Dame costumes and props. I was at my wit's end when I got back to Linden Gardens.

Jennifer O'List came to my rescue. 'I'll help you,' she said. And God bless her, she managed to come up with a couple of comedy dresses which she made herself from material she borrowed from the Windmill wardrobe, even providing me with the props for the 'knitting' gag.

The show opened on Boxing Day, and Myra and I spent Christmas Day with Mam and Dad who were staying with Fred and his wife in Machen, outside Newport. We walked miles with our cases that night, unable to get a taxi, and we were about half a mile from the station before we got a lift.

The opening night from my point of view was a disaster. My wig fell off in one scene, causing the kids to cry out in disappointment, 'It's a man – it's a man!' although it must have been pretty obvious from the start that I was no lady. I thought it would be rather funny if I appeared in one scene with a false moustache and a cigar à la Groucho Marx, but the audience was not happy about their beloved traditions being tampered with. Hal Blue, the comedian playing Idle Jack, helped me through the bits of business which I had found so mystifying at rehearsal, but the applause I received in the final walk-down at the end of the performance was lukewarm.

I was sitting in my dressing-room taking off my make-up while Myra tried to reassure me that I was not all that bad when the door opened and the man who was financially responsible for putting on the pantomime stood in the doorway. Apparently he was not a very well man and my performance had not helped his condition. He shook a finger at me for a full minute, trembling with rage as he sought to utter the words to express his feelings. I stood up, out of respect, ready for the tirade which never came – he was the first man I had ever come across who was actually speechless with rage. Charles King, the director, led him away by the arm, still wordless. I wondered what it was about me that could arouse such strong passion in some people – the owner of the Grand Theatre, Bolton, and now this chap. I had a feeling that there would be many more like them before I finished in show business.

It was obviously too late to get a replacement for me in the pantomime, and gradually I began to enjoy myself. Things were constantly going wrong with the production and I have always thrived on disaster.

The 'knitting gag' turned out to be quite a simple piece of business. When I made my first entrance, usually in a blaze of indifference, I carried on stage with me a shopping basket which contained two giant knitting needles from which hung a half-finished woollen scarf. I told the audience that I was going to hang my basket on a nail on the side of the stage and that if anybody went to touch it they were to shout, 'Put that down!' (Really sophisticated stuff, as I'm sure you have gathered.)

Unfortunately, I could not always find the nail in the proscenium arch owing to my short-sightedness, and after fumbling for it, I would more often than not leave the basket on the floor, where everybody coming on from that side would trip over it, particularly my friend, the cat. He used to complain bitterly about it, but one matinée he caused quite a bit of excitement himself.

It was the Highgate Hill sequence where Dick Whittington did a soliloquy with Tom, the cat, who was supposed to appear on the cue 'But I still have Tom, my faithful friend'. Delyse delivered the line, but no Tom appeared. She repeated the cue, adding a few extra lines under her breath which did not augur well for the cat after the show. Meanwhile, Tom, who was rather deaf, had forgotten to turn up the loudspeaker in his dressing-room and at the very moment when his big scene was about to unfold was sitting down with his cat's head off, drinking a glass of stout.

The assistant stage-manager raced up the stairs and banged on his door to tell him he had missed his cue. Tom was so confused that he rushed down the stairs and on to the stage without his cat's head. The sight of a bald cat standing upright sent the audience into shock and Dick into hysterics.

Incidentally, this happened at Walthamstow, a place which features in one of the funniest ad libs I've ever heard. Charles Henry, a producer I had the good fortune of working with later on at the Palladium, was once asked how he thought 'Goodnight Vienna' would go down in Walthamstow. His reply was: 'About as well as "Goodnight Walthamstow" would go down in Vienna.'

Towards the end of the tour things began to deteriorate and props would go wrong quite regularly. In one scene the Demon Rat had to sink the ship upon which we were sailing to Malabar. He did this by pointing dramatically at the left side of the ship's bridge where a couple of powder flashes were concealed, and declaiming, 'I'll sink this ship. Come, fire!' Then the flashes would go off. Turning, he would then point at the right side of the bridge and say, 'Come, thunder!' And two more flashes would rend the air.

Unfortunately, one afternoon at the Chelsea Palace, after a hearty lunch, the Demon Rat became slightly confused and got his moves the wrong way round. Instead of pointing first to the left, he pointed to the right, and received a fairly hefty charge of powder flash up the back of his tights. If he'd stayed where he was and indicated the right side again, he'd have been all right. However, unnerved by his singed backside, he turned and pointed left, and got the second charge full in the rear. He clutched his backside and cried, 'Bollocks!' Then he limped painfully off stage. The kids loved it.

There was a speciality act about half-way through the pantomime which was quite bizarre. It opened with a man in a striped blazer and carrying a tennis racquet walking on stage backwards into a dining-room set. A large table laid for a dozen guests, with a candelabra in the middle, was situated centre stage. The man did a few tricks with the tennis racquet, and then on came a dwarf dressed as Hitler in a tin hat. He marched up and down for a while, and was followed on stage by a lady in a short, fringed jacket and tights carrying a saxophone, upon which she began to play 'Smoke Gets In Your Eyes'. In the background the man in the striped blazer was preparing himself to lift the table into the air. He always appeared to have difficulty, and on some nights the tiny Hitler and the lady saxophonist would go to his assistance. The climax of the act was when he balanced the table on his chin by one of its legs. The candelabra would then light up and all three would take their applause. Sometimes the light would refuse to go on, and together they'd put the table back on stage and the man in the striped blazer would work underneath it with a screwdriver. Meanwhile, the lady saxophonist would play another few choruses of 'Smoke Gets In Your Eyes' until her partner announced that he was ready to try again. It was the most surreal performance I have ever seen, and made Pinter's *The Birthday Party* seem like *Postman Pat*. I never failed to watch it.

After the pantomime had finished I got a couple of dates in northern variety theatres. I was very anxious to put something in the bank, because I had fixed the biggest date of my life – my marriage to Myra. 19 February 1948 was to see the union of Harry Donald Secombe and Myra Joan Atherton, spinster, but there wasn't much in the kitty.

Then I was offered a contract for a touring revue to do 'act as known' and 'appear as required in sketches' at a salary of forty pounds a week. This was the lifeline I had been praying for and meant that I'd be in regular employment for at least six months after we'd come back from our honeymoon.

The day of the wedding was sunny but chilly. Myra's wedding dress was made by her Aunty Elsie from six yards of material, which was all that was allowed in those days of rationing. It had a heart-shaped neckline and she wore her grandmother's pearls. My suit came off the peg. We were married in St Barnabas Church, Sketty, Swansea, and my brother Fred performed the ceremony. When it came to the part of the service which goes 'with this ring I thee wed', I was about to put the ring on the wrong finger. 'The third one, you idiot!' whispered the Reverend Fred. My sister, Carol, was one of Myra's two bridesmaids, and Carol's fiancé, Josh Williams, whom she married the following April, was my best man. The other bridesmaid was Myra's cousin, Beryl Atherton.

Ronnie Bridges came down from London for the occasion, and while we were waiting for the bride to make her entrance he played 'I'm Just Wild About Harry' in the style of a Bach fugue.

After the church service all the principals went off to Chapman's, the photographic studio, for the mandatory wedding pictures, and there was a reception for seventy-five people at the Glanmor Country Club. There's posh for you.

Myra's Dad, who really was unaccustomed to public speaking, made an excellent short speech and a good time was had by all. We caught the five o'clock train from High Street Station for Bristol, our night-stop on the way to Penzance for our week's honeymoon. Ronnie Bridges travelled in our compartment as far as Cardiff, and when he left the train he was so covered in confetti he looked like a bridegroom who had mislaid his bride.

We had a slap-up meal in the hotel and retired early. That night it snowed, but I must confess we didn't notice.

We had chosen Penzance because it was as far as we could go without actually going abroad. Travel overseas was restricted and I don't think we could have afforded a continental trip anyway. At least there were palm trees on the front, even though they were being blown all over the place in the wet, windy weather when we first arrived. We seemed always to be last down to breakfast in the hotel – a fact which occasioned a few smiles. We walked for miles in the surrounding countryside, getting to know each other and generally having a great time. Need I say more? I decided then that if marriage is a lottery, I held a winning ticket.

When the honeymoon was over we went to London to stay in digs in Kensal Rise for the rehearsal period of the new show I was joining. I was told to report to a church hall in Clapham for my first day with the new company, and had difficulty finding the place. When I did find it, I thought I had made a mistake. Lots of young men wearing ladies' clothes were cavorting around to music which came from a battered piano. I went back outside, found a call box and phoned the agent who had booked me for the job.

'You've given me the wrong address,' I said, laughing at his mistake. 'There's a whole bunch of fellers dressed like women dancing around in there.'

'That's right,' said the agent. 'The show's called *Forces Showboat* and it's a drag show.'

'Oh dear,' I said. 'Look, I hope I'm not expected to dress up like that, I've just got married.'

It was the agent's turn to laugh. 'Don't worry, I saw you play Dame at the Chelsea Palace, remember? You're just doing your act and appearing as yourself in a couple of quick blackout sketches.' And he put the phone down.

I swallowed hard and went back into the church hall to rehearse. After all, I needed the money.

Topping the bill was a double act called Bartlett and Ross, female impersonators who were seasoned professionals with immaculate timing that was a joy to watch. Colin Ross, who never looked right in men's clothes, took a fancy to Myra and used to go shopping with her. His partner, Terry Bartlett, had a good singing voice.

It was the singing in my act which bothered me at first, especially the Jeanette MacDonald impersonation, so I began to blow a veritable hurricane of raspberries in case anybody got the wrong idea about me. The rest of the company thought this was extremely funny, especially one young lad called Danny Carroll, whom Myra took under her wing because she felt that he was a cut above the rest of the chorus boys. He was – and Danny La Rue always makes a big fuss over Myra whenever we meet.

I was still doing radio broadcasts on the odd Sunday and was involved in trial recordings for two separate BBC comedy series. One of them, called 'Get Going', got nowhere, but another, produced by an avant garde veteran of comedy, Pat Dixon, was taken up. It was called 'Listen, My Children' and featured Robert Beatty, Carol Carr, Patricia Hayes, Benny Hill, Bennie Lee, Jon Pertwee, and the Vic Lewis Orchestra. The writers were Paul Dehn, Frank Muir and Denis Norden. It was way ahead of its time, as was Pat Dixon, a tall professorial type with thick spectacles who operated from a room in the rabbit warren that was Aeolian Hall in Bond Street. The walls of his office were lined with hundreds of files and books about comedy. He was a great enthusiast and gathered around him a stable of young comedians who shared that enthusiasm. He would go into paroxysms of laughter reading pieces from the Canadian humorist Stephen Leacock's book *Literary Lapses* and he knew the dialogue of all the Marx Brothers' films.

The pilot, or trial recording, for 'Listen, My Children' led to a series of eight programmes and the first one was broadcast on the BBC Home Service on 1 June 1948.

Between broadcasts and *Forces Showboat* appearances I spent a lot of time at Grafton's with Mike and all the other comics who used to congregate in the saloon bar until the early hours of the morning, intoxicated not only with what we'd been drinking, but also with each other's company. Dick Emery would be there and the bar would ring with the uninhibited laughter of Bill Kerr and Spike as they exchanged filthy army jokes.

Incidentally, the second time I went along to see Jimmy Grafton at the pub I was on my own and went into the saloon bar for a drink and a chat. When I ordered my half pint of mild – business was bad at the time – he smiled, handed over the beer and moved away without saying a word.

I was rather hurt by his behaviour because Jimmy and I had enjoyed such a great evening the previous week, so I took my drink and sat alone in a corner of the bar. Then he came up to me, made a big fuss of me and asked me what I was going to have to drink. Puzzled, I indicated my half pint of mild and reminded him that he had only just served me.

'That wasn't me,' he laughed. 'That was Peter, my twin brother.' And he called over the person I could have sworn was Jimmy.

They really were identical twins and were extremely difficult to tell apart. Years later I remember Peter turning up at a party for Jimmy in Melbourne wearing the same patterned cravat and practically identical sports jacket and trousers as his twin – and they hadn't seen each other for about three months.

Myra and I went on touring around the halls with *Forces Showboat*, staying in some strange lodgings along the way. There was one landlady in Plymouth who would come into our bedroom with the breakfast tray and then stay talking until eleven o'clock, telling us all about her ailments and how badly they'd been bombed in the war, and we couldn't get a word in edgeways. I used to fall asleep in the middle of the conversation and wake up to find her still yapping on and my bladder bursting.

Theatrical landladies were a strange breed. They always had tickets for the first house on the Monday and if they didn't like your act, you'd suffer for the rest of the week. One old dear would just thump my meal on the table in front of me, sniff loudly and walk out of the room mumbling, 'Call yourself a comic.' But if the landlady took a fancy to you it was roses all the way for the week.

Once when I was sharing digs with Norman Vaughan we had a letter from Les Henry, a comedian who had been in one of the Central Pool of Artists shows in Italy, and later became 'Cedric' in the comedy harmonica act, the Three Monarchs. He had heard that these particular digs were good and asked us to fix him up there the following week.

We wrote back saying that we had booked him a room, but offered him a bit of friendly advice about the landlady. We told him that she was very deaf, but out of pride refused to wear a deaf aid, so it would be a good idea if he spoke loudly when addressing her. There was, of course, nothing wrong with her hearing at all.

What he didn't know was that we had told her the same thing about him, and by the Thursday of the week he was staying with her, he had lost his voice completely. It was only when he started writing down instructions to her on a writing pad that they both realized the joke we had played on them.

There was one very nice landlady in Halifax who, while perched on the loo one morning, became aware that she was being watched through a knot-hole in the door. She recognized the eye as belonging to one of her week's lodgers – a randy old stage-manager with an unsavoury reputation. That particular time she was unable to do anything about the Peeping Tom. However, the following morning she went into the toilet well prepared. She waited until the eye made its appearances and jabbed at it with a knitting needle she had taken in with her. There was a horrible yell and she heard the stage-manager – for it was he – stumble up the stairs. He turned up that evening for his dinner with his eye heavily bandaged, but never a word was spoken about the incident.

To get back to the *Forces Showboat* tour, there was one awful week Myra and I suffered when the show was playing Harrow in North London. The landlady of the digs which had been recommended had to turn us down at the last minute, and we finished up on the Sunday night at an evil-smelling house in a back street. The character who ran the place was straight out of a Dickens novel, hatchet-faced and dressed in black. She informed us that she was doing us a favour by letting us have her best room. After she had shown us into the room, Myra said in a whisper – because it was that kind of atmosphere – 'If this is the best room, what must the others look like?'

A naked bulb hung from the ceiling, and the flimsy wardrobe had a door that wouldn't stay shut. There was bare linoleum on the floor, and the bed was a single one. Myra refused to unpack any of our clothes and we were so cold we had to put our dressing-gowns on to go to bed. During the night some drunk began banging on the door asking to be let in, and it was some time before he went away.

At breakfast the next morning our hostess informed us over a cup of tea in which grease floated, that her real job was laying out the corpses in the local mortuary, and she regaled us with some jolly tales of the vicissitudes of her profession.

When Myra and I left for the band call we took one of the suitcases containing my stage suit and props, leaving behind the cabin trunk which held my street clothes and Myra's dresses and shoes.

Fortunately, that afternoon I met a friend of ours from the Windmill days – Barry Brigg, an RAF pilot who had married Daddy Allen's daughter. When we told him of our experiences of the previous night, he said, 'For God's sake don't go back there, come home and stay with us – June will be delighted to see you.'

We gladly accepted the offer and the following morning Myra went back to the digs to pay what we owed and retrieve our trunk.

She found the door to our room locked and a huge padlock and chain had been fastened outside. The landlady refused to let her in to get the luggage until the week's rent had been paid. Myra came back to the Briggs' house with the news, and I had to go down from the theatre, where I had been rehearsing, to claim the trunk. When I gave the woman the money she unchained the door and I took the trunk away.

There was a strong sense of evil in that house, and in order not to be caught out again I applied to the Actors' Church Union for their list of recommended accommodation for actors. We found it extremely useful and it became our 'bible' when we were on tour. Appropriate, really.

All the time I had been working in *Forces Showboat* and doing the odd radio or television broadcast, I never considered singing seriously. If I sang at all, it was always in a burlesque way, because I was so concerned with being a comedian that I had no real desire to add a straight song to the act. I was afraid of using my voice in a serious way in case I got laughs in the wrong places. Anyway, it was a big, untrained voice, liable to go out of tune when under pressure – although in the bath I sang like a dream. However, the more often I broadcast on 'Variety Bandbox', the harder it became to find enough material to fill in the time, and it was always good to have a finish to your act. Some comics closed with a monologue or a tap dance like Norman Vaughan – but tap dancing on radio was obviously out. Arthur English had a unique way of finishing his performance when he did a stint on 'Variety Bandbox'. He would get louder and louder and faster and faster and then shout 'Open the cage!' as a way of getting applause. Reg Dixon, a resident on 'Variety Bandbox', would sing 'Confidentially' to open his act, and end with a ballad of some kind, but the only comedian who sang in a full-throated way was Issy Bonn. Some of the older pros had good voices – people like Tommy Handley, Stanley

Holloway and Arthur Askey all used their vocal ability to bolster their performances.

Jimmy Grafton was all for me doing the same. 'Try a song to finish with on your next "Bandbox",' he suggested. 'You've got one coming up in October.'

I decided to have a go at it and picked a song which seemed to suit my voice. It was called 'When You're In Love', and was a Spanish song, originally entitled 'La Paloma', to which English words had been added.

Myra and I were staying in digs in Brixton at this time. She was expecting our first child, something that didn't stop her doing cartwheels in the street on the way home from the theatre the evening after her pregnancy was confirmed. But now she was suffering from morning sickness and wasn't feeling too well. The week before the broadcast in which I was to sing my first straight ballad, we had very little money left and we'd used up all the meat coupons on our ration books. We lived on potatoes for several days – fried, boiled, and in their jackets. Sketching had always been a favourite pastime of mine, and I became preoccupied with drawing heads and flowers and God knows what else with a soft-leaded pencil all over the marble mantelpiece in our room in the digs. The landlady, Mrs Rattray, was used to the eccentricities of her theatrical guests and didn't mind at all, but I have no doubt that she wiped the lot off as soon as we had gone.

On the day of the 'Variety Bandbox' broadcast, I went along to the band call with a full orchestration of 'When You're In Love' provided for me by the publishers. The conductor, Billy Ternant, who knew me by now from previous shows, was very patient with my fumbling attempts to come to terms with the music. It sounded very different from the simple piano part and I had trouble sorting out exactly where to come in. In the end he got the pianist in the orchestra to give me a bell note when it was time for me to start.

Jimmy Grafton was very keen that I didn't muck about with the song. 'No going cross-eyed in the middle or anything like that,' he admonished in the dressing-room before I went on. I didn't. When I came to the end of the comedy routine Jim had written, I announced the song, and sang it straight, all the way through. However, at the end, after I had got the top note, I fell flat on my back. It was my way of compromising. It was a start, though, and it gave me enough confidence to begin to think of adding a straight song every time I did a radio show.

It wasn't always successful, however. After one programme Stanley Black, the conductor, said to me. 'Do you know that you sang "Granada" all the way through a quarter of a tone sharp?'

I looked at him and said, 'Do you think it's easy?'

He threw his baton at me.

Christmas 1948 was a traumatic time for Myra and me. *Forces Showboat* was playing Bristol the week before Christmas and everybody was looking forward to going home for the festivities. However, on the Friday when we were supposed to be paid, the man responsible for financing the show had no money, and the company was stranded. It was like something out of a Hollywood musical, with tears being shed all around, everybody looking very desperate, and me with a pregnant wife. Fortunately I knew a man in Bristol who had taken a liking to Myra and myself and I managed, with his help, to get enough money to pay the train fare home for the company. Bill Pavey was his name, and I am eternally grateful to him.

We spent Christmas at home with Myra's parents and had a great time. Even though we had experienced the worst thing that can happen to a performer, apart from being taken off the bill – and I'd already been through that – I felt that things were getting brighter. I had a radio series with Pat Dixon to come in the New Year, and on New Year's Day I had a television show to do – another *Rooftop Rendezvous*.

The radio series I was contracted to do was 'Third Division', and Pat had gathered around him a team which would take some beating. Robert Beatty headed the cast, and other members of 'Listen, My Children' were also included – Bennie Lee, Pat Hayes, Benny Hill and myself. The newcomers were Bruce Belfrage, Michael Bentine and Peter Sellers. This was the first time that Mike, Peter and I had worked together and was a forerunner for 'The Goon Show'. The comedy was thought to be too way-out for Light Programme listeners and went out on the Third Programme – the equivalent of today's Radio 3.

Naturally, Mike and I took Peter along to Grafton's. He was so obviously one of us and his repertoire of impressions was formidable. Like the rest of us, he had been in the services and shared our lunatic sense of humour. Spike and Peter took to each other immediately and soon the four of us were meeting regularly.

Rooftop Rendezvous on New Year's Day 1949 was a live television programme – as they all were in those days – and was broadcast from the Alexandra Palace Studios. I was required to wear full evening dress for my act, and that was the cause of some concern because I didn't possess it. Fortunately a fellow lodger at Mrs Rattray's knew somebody who worked at the theatrical costumiers, Fox's. 'He'll fix you up with a really good outfit,' he said. 'Just tell him I sent you.'

Of course, when I went along to Fox's the lodger's friend was not there, and the selection of evening wear was very poor – all the good stuff had already gone out. 'Christmas and the New Year is a busy time for us,' explained the assistant who served me. 'Have a look through this lot.'

I eventually chose a tail jacket which was too long and a pair of trousers which were too short and which turned out to have a greenish tinge under the studio lights. Seeing my disappointment, the assistant let me have the dress shirt and waistcoat for nothing. 'But don't forget to bring the lot back on time,' he said, pocketing the thirty shillings I gave him. I was only getting ten guineas for the show.

As a change from the shaving act I had worked out a routine of how different people ate sandwiches – the hungry man, the laughing nibbler, the man who was allergic to mustard, and a couple of others I've forgotten now. I had asked for very thin sandwiches so that I wouldn't have too much in my mouth at any one time, otherwise I would not be able to speak.

'You shall have them – don't worry, old chap,' said the floor manager cheerfully. (That always makes me suspicious – give me a floor manager who worries, I always say.)

There was no time for a proper dress run-through, and when the red light came on in the studio, signalling the start of the show, I still hadn't seen the sandwiches I was to use in the act. I was also having trouble keeping my starched shirt front in position. It was not a proper shirt; the collar, the bow tie and the starched front part with the three black studs, were all one piece, fastened at the bottom by a tab which fitted over a button in the top of my trousers. I have a long torso, and the fake shirt front was too short. It was all right when I bent forward, but when I straightened up, the tab attached to my pants was under great strain and put my manhood in jeopardy.

They had placed me in a corner of the set, seated at a table, and the idea was that a waiter came on, put a plate of sandwiches before me and left me to it. The band struck up my signature tune – 'I'm Just Wild About Harry' – and the waiter duly appeared bearing a plate of six of the biggest doorstep sandwiches I'd ever seen. When they were placed before me it was obvious that they had been left under the lights somewhere and, big as they were, they were curling at the edges.

There was nothing I could do but go into the routine – this was live television. I announced the first sandwich eater – the very hungry one – and began stuffing the dry bread into my mouth. It was a horrible experience, and as I progressed I was spitting bread everywhere. The effort of trying to bend forward to keep the pressure off my groin was getting unbearable, and when I eventually came to the 'laughing nibbler' bit I was forced to straighten up. The tab on my shirt front snapped and the whole lot unrolled upwards like a blind, revealing an expanse of bare, sweating flesh. The band went hysterical and the camera swung away from me. I thought I had blown my chance of becoming a TV star for good, but the producer came around to my dressing-room afterwards and congratulated me. 'Sheer genius, that bit with the shirt front,' he said. 'I thought the act was going downhill at one point, and then you produced that glorious piece of business. Beautifully timed. Congratulations.'

I went home on the bus from Alexandra Palace that night determined to try that same 'piece of business' in my act, and then in the cold light of a Brixton morning I realized that there was no way I could ever repeat that completely unrehearsed moment.

On some occasions, however, it is possible. Fourteen years later, during the trial scene in the musical *Pickwick*, I accidentally broke off the wooden bar which formed the front part of the dock I was standing in. I looked so surprised that the audience laughed uproariously. It was such a good reaction and, coming at a dramatic part of the play, relieved the tension at just the right moment, so I thought I'd try to do it again on purpose the following night. I arranged for the bar to be loosely attached to its moorings and when the time came I broke it off deliberately in the same way I had done it accidentally the night before. It worked again, for some reason, and it stayed in for the rest of the run. People would come up to me and say, 'I was in the audience the night when you broke off the wooden bar on the dock.' And I'd nod and smile, but I never let on.

CHAPTER NINE

New Responsibilities

I had quite a lot of radio shows in the first couple of months of 1949 – 'Third Division' was going out, and on 26 January I did a trial recording for the 'Cyril Fletcher Show'. Cyril had a regular summer season at the Pavilion Theatre, Torquay, and was looking for a comedian. To my delight I got the job, probably on the strength of the broadcast, and the summer looked nice and secure. There were to be a couple of weeks in Hastings at the White Rock Pavilion, a further two at the Knightstone Pavilion, Weston-super-Mare, and a short run at the Theatre Royal, Bath, after the Torquay season. In addition, there were to be some television appearances in Cyril's own show. All this meant that Myra and I could look forward to the arrival of our first child knowing that I would be getting a steady weekly wage.

As I have already mentioned, radio did not pay much. My fee was ten guineas at the time, so I had to fill in with as many theatrical dates as I could. My act was getting more polished – I suppose you could say that I was being fired in the crucible of the music halls. It was the proud boast of the stage door-keeper of every theatre up north that 'If yer can please 'em 'ere you'll please 'em anywhere.'

Once, as I left the stage door of the Theatre Royal, Barnsley, a cloth-capped gentleman grasped my arm firmly and informed me, 'You nearly 'ad me laughing when you were on, lad.' And he meant it as a compliment.

Discipline was always strict in the better-class venues – the Moss Empires and Stoll Theatres – but it was also rigidly applied in the smaller establishments. If you went over your allotted time by too many minutes you were in trouble with head office. The stage-manager put down on his report sheet the time you went on stage and the time you came off, and stage-managers were unbribable. There was no excuse for coming late to work either – every artist had to be in his dressing-room by the time the half-hour was called by the stage-manager. There was also a rule that no fish and chips were to be brought into the theatre.

I was not aware of this, and one Friday night when I was playing a northern Palace, I went out to the chip shop down the road and brought back a couple of bob's worth of cod and fried potatoes. The stage door-keeper was on the phone when I got back, and obviously didn't notice me enter. I was in the middle of my meal in the dressing-room when I heard the thundering cry come up the stairs, 'Who's eating bloody chips in 'ere?'

The accordionist in the next room to mine rushed in and started wafting the air with a towel. 'I thought it was you,' she said. She pointed to the window. 'There's a ledge you can stand on out there.'

Without thinking I climbed out of the window and stood on a rather narrow ledge, with the remains of my supper in one hand. When I looked down I nearly fainted. Because of my lowly position on the bill, I was on the third floor. The star had the stage-level dressing-room and the lesser acts ascended the building in order of size of billing. I was lucky not to be on the roof. I've never had a head for heights, and I spent a very uncomfortable few minutes clinging to the brickwork around the window until the accordionist announced the all-clear. I never did it again.

*

The week that Myra was expecting our baby to arrive I was playing Feldman's Theatre, Blackpool, and she was at home in Swansea with her parents. I had been down at the weekend but had to leave on the Sunday to be in Blackpool for band call on Monday morning.

There were two comics on the bill. I was one of them, and the other was a young ex-serviceman who had been in the RAF *Gang Show*. Tony Hancock was a slim, nervous lad in those days – as was I – and we had a lot in common. We had met at Daddy Allen's Club and he was a frequent visitor to Jimmy Grafton's pub in Westminster. His act was completely different from mine, but like Peter and Mike he spurned the 'string of gags' approach to comedy, and among other things he did an impression of a British Movietone Newsreel.

As I came off stage after my first performance that Monday night, 11 April 1949, the stage-manager said there was a phone call for me. I rushed up the stairs to the manager's office, my face full of shaving soap, to receive the news that Myra had given birth to a six-and-a-half-pound baby girl. I was over the moon with delight and asked Tony to join me in a drink and a meal after the second house.

By the time we had both cleaned up, all the pubs were shut and the only place open was a fish and chip bar down a side street. Over our steaming fried haddock and sixpennyworth of chips we toasted my new daughter's health in a couple of glasses of Tizer. Then we walked down to the promenade, leaned over the rails, and discussed our futures. We were young and ambitious and the night seemed strangely full of promise as we looked down into the dark water, seeing only stars there. I shall always remember Tony as he was then, before the drink got the better of him. He was uncertain of himself and talked a lot about the art of comedy, especially about Sid Field, upon whom he was beginning to model himself. He was not content just to accept the laughs he got for a piece of 'business', he wanted to know why the audience found him funny. I was always only too ready to take the reward without questioning it too closely. Tony never was, and eventually embarked on a quest for perfection that led him to get rid of all the stalwarts who worked with him on his radio and TV shows.

As I was to write much later in a foreword to a book about Tony written by his widow, Freddie Ross, together with David Nathan: 'The demands of his profession shaped him, ground him down and eventually killed him, but he served it well. If anyone paid dearly for his laughs, it was the lad himself. May he lie sweetly at rest.'

I couldn't wait to get back to Swansea at the weekend to see the new baby. She had a mop of black hair like her mother, and big, dark brown eyes like her mother, but by God she had my lungs. Seeing her I realized that I now had increased responsibilities, and as yet Myra and I had no home of our own. It was time I started to get enough money together to buy one.

I travelled to Cardiff on 13 May to record 'Welsh Rarebit', a long-running variety show which had a high listening figure, and I was keen to make an impression. The producer was Mai Jones, a lady of tremendous energy and talent who also conducted the orchestra. Her husband, Dai, was the programme's engineer.

Mai went through the script I had brought along, looking for innuendoes, putting her pencil through the odd line. 'Mustn't have anything naughty on "Welsh Rarebit", love,' she said. What she had crossed out was a reference to a 'district nurse'. I could not see what harm there was in it but as it was my first 'Rarebit' I kept my mouth shut. At least she allowed me one raspberry.

We then ran over the music and Mai made some helpful suggestions about how I should handle the song. It was 'Falling In Love With Love', which had been made famous by Alan Jones, the Hollywood musical star whom I admired very much. My reputation had gone before me, and as I went into the number she wagged her baton at me. 'No making funny faces in the middle, now.' I promised to try to sing it properly – and I did. The result was that I became a regular item on 'Welsh Rarebit' for the next few years, and it helped to build my career. The theme song, 'We'll Keep A Welcome', for which Mai wrote the music, has been a feature of my stage act as long as I can remember, and if I don't sing it I get complaints.

The shows were recorded in Corey Hall in Cardiff, a place with excellent acoustics and ideal for the purpose of broadcasting. However, it had one unfortunate drawback – there were no toilets backstage. Quite a number of the cast members were getting on a bit, especially the actors who were involved in the regular 'Tommy Trouble' feature, and after a few pints they would begin to feel very uncomfortable. There must have been a few bladders ruptured in the cause of radio, until a bucket was provided for surreptitious relief in the corner of the dressing-room.

It was a great show to do and I made many friends, including Frank James, the compère, Alun Williams, the announcer, comedians Wyn Calvin and Stan Stennet, Albert and Les Ward, a comedy musical act, and Ossie Morris. Ossie was a naturally funny man to whom fame came late in life. For years he had worked in the steelworks at Port Talbot and performed locally as an amateur, until Mai Jones discovered him. He had a good singing voice and his gimmick of 'I must 'ave 'ush' became a popular catch-phrase of the day. Another regular who became a star in middle age via 'Welsh Rarebit' was Gladys Morgan, a dear lady with a high-pitched cackle.

The programme also gave me an opportunity to work alongside some of the top singers and comedians of the day. Donald Peers was very popular at that time and I used to watch in awe as he stood among his fans, signing autographs with a flourish, his overcoat draped over his shoulders in the manner of a Continental film star. I wondered if ever I'd get to that stage, and even practised the overcoat bit, but it always fell off.

Although Mai discovered a lot of future stars, there was one who slipped through the net. A young singer once auditioned for her and was told to 'go home, love' – and Shirley Bassey went back, temporarily, to Tiger Bay.

The television series of Cyril Fletcher's show went very well and I was given plenty of work in the sketches, although I had no singing to do. I had a couple of good notices in the press and I was looking forward to the rehearsals for the summer show, which was called *Magpie Masquerade*.

It was a sumptuously dressed seaside revue, and the men wore full evening dress for the opening and the finale. Betty Astell, Cyril's wife, wore crinolines and wonderful beaded and sequinned gowns which she made herself, and the ladies of the company dressed in the height of fashion.

I had never been in a show of this kind before, and I felt a bit like a fish out of water. However, I was determined to make the most of it.

Myra had answered an advertisement for a cottage to rent in Brixham, a fishing village not too far from Torquay which could be reached quite quickly by a converted motor torpedo boat which plied between the two harbours.

We had no car as yet, and Myra came down from Swansea on the train with her mother, all our luggage, a pram, and three-month-old Jennifer. We had liked Reg O'List's wife's name so much that we decided to call our first-born after her.

The scene was now set for what should have been a glorious summer season, but it didn't quite turn out that way. For a start, Cyril was a laid-back comedian whose humour was gentle, as witness his 'odd odes' which made him famous on radio. My approach to comedy was still rather rough and ready, and I had not yet learned the art of subtlety – especially when performing in the sketches. I was apt to ad lib when the fancy took me, and after a Guinness or two, my raspberries got fruitier.

For the show's finale, all the male members of the company had to stand in line and unfurl opera cloaks, revealing their crimson linings, as Betty came down the staircase to take her bow. On one occasion I thought it would be a great idea to write 'Eat at Joe's' on the inside of my cloak. The laugh I got when the message was revealed completely spoiled poor Betty's entrance, and I was quite rightly given a severe telling-off.

There was another scene, set in Bath, in which the whole company was dressed in elegant Georgian costumes. Betty sang a song and we finished with a number called 'Oh Listen To The Band', the last lines of which went, 'To the shouts of here we come, and the banging of the drum, Oh listen to the music in the park.' However, I got into the habit of singing slightly different words to the real ones. One night, the rest of the cast – on the instructions of Nugent Marshall, who had been at the Windmill when I was there and had a wicked sense of humour – stopped singing before they came to the afore-mentioned lines. The result was that the audience heard, 'To the shouts of here we come, put your finger up your bum, and listen to the music in the park,' sung as a solo by yours truly. Actually, I thought I sang it rather well, but Cyril and Betty did not appreciate my efforts.

To be honest, Cyril didn't know how to handle me, and, looking back, I would have felt the same if some zany young idiot had started messing about in one of my summer shows. His only complaint to my agent was that I was rather 'robust', an understatement if ever there was one. Cyril and I have discussed the show since and had a good laugh about it, but it wasn't too good an experience for either of us at the time. I was a misfit in the elegant atmosphere of the concert party. There were still traces of the NAAFI performer in me, and my overdeveloped sense of the ridiculous kept getting me into trouble.

Back at the cottage in Brixham, Myra was having difficulty with Jennifer, who seemed to be crying incessantly for no apparent reason. It was lonely for Myra being stuck on her own when I was out every night doing the show, but she never complained, God bless her.

I thought it was time that I bought a car – it might cheer everybody up. Gordon Holdom, the baritone in *Magpie Masquerade*, had a car which he said I could have for forty pounds. I snapped up his offer. It was an old Humber – a very old Humber – but it had the look of having been a great car at one time. Perhaps it had belonged to someone of substance – at any rate it now belonged to someone of very little substance, because the forty quid nearly cleaned me out.

The first difficulty I encountered was the fact that although I had driven all sorts of vehicles in the the war, including a Bren carrier, I had forgotten to renew the licence I had been given by Major Sims back in Usk in 1939. Consequently I had to take the driving test again. This was a blow, because I now had a car but was unable to drive it. I could see the damned thing parked down at the quayside, slowly disintegrating before my very eyes.

I decided to apply right away for a test, and obtained a provisional licence. As a refresher I fixed up a crash course of driving lessons – very appropriately termed, as it turned out. When my driving instructor arrived I found, to my surprise, that he had only one arm. I showed him what I could do and he pronounced that I would have no difficulty whatsoever in passing the test. We then adjourned to the pub.

The following week I took my driving test, thanks to the influence of my one-armed friend. He and I went out for a quick drive before the examination, which was arranged for two o'clock that afternoon. Afterwards we adjourned to the pub again and I had a couple of bottles of Guinness.

It was a very hot afternoon, and I parked the car outside the place where I was supposed to meet the examiner, about half an hour before the appointment. I put my head back against the seat and dozed. The next thing I knew was that a hand was shaking me awake. The examiner was anxious to get going, and after checking my name and particulars on his clipboard, he told me to proceed. He watched patiently as I tried to start the car. The Humber was a slow starter and I was beginning to despair of the ignition ever firing, but finally it clattered into life. I smiled at him in relief, put the car smartly into reverse and moved backwards into a parked bicycle. As I got out to see if the bike was damaged – fortunately it was not – I saw the examiner writing something down on his clipboard.

Torquay is a town of many hills, and I chatted away desperately as I tried to coax the old banger to negotiate some of them – and all the time the examiner was writing away on his clipboard. The climax came when, attempting a flashy three-point turn, I drove inexorably into the back of a stationary bus. The examiner got out, grim-faced, and, giving me a yellow slip, announced that I had failed on everything.

'You didn't try me on the Highway Code,' I said plaintively. 'I'm good on that.'

But he had gone, leaving me to deal with an irate bus driver. I drove back to my driving instructor's office on my own, which afterwards I realized was quite illegal because every learner has to have a licensed driver alongside him.

The instructor was quite surprised that I'd failed the test. 'Pity he didn't try you on the Highway Code,' he said in an attempt to mollify me. 'You're good on that. Never mind, better luck next time.' And we adjourned to the pub.

I did pass the second time, a few weeks later, but the old car was on its last legs and I used the one-armed gent's vehicle for the test. When I came to drive the Humber regularly I found that if I went over twenty miles an hour the perspex windows of the two rear doors slowly wound down, with the result that anyone who rode in it eventually finished up with a head cold. Myra's parents would sit in the back seat wrapped up like Scotts of the Antarctic.

When we finished the season in Bath I tried hard to sell the car. At one point I was about to secure the deal at a garage, but made the fatal mistake of taking my foot off the accelerator with which I was keeping the mortally wounded engine alive. It died immediately I did so and nothing could revive it. The garage owner, who was about to pay me twenty pounds for it, subsequently charged me five pounds for having it towed away.

The rest of the year was pretty quiet with only a few broadcasts, mostly 'Variety Bandbox' shows, and a sprinkling of theatre dates. My only television appearance was on 23 December when I played the Judge in *Toad Of Toad Hall*, which went out live from Alexandra Palace. The cast was excellent, with Cameron Hall as Toad, Kenneth More as Badger, Jill Balcon the Narrator, Andrew Osborne as Ratty, Jack Newmark as Mole, and Desmond Walter Ellis as the Usher. Sam Kydd, with whom I had toured Germany in the show with Peter Waring, was one of the water rats, and Oscar Quitack, who was to play Mr Winkle to my Pickwick much later on, was the back-end of the horse.

I welcomed the opportunity to work with actors and found them all very generous. My part as the Judge in the courtroom scene required me to sing a song as well as deliver quite a lot of dialogue. There was one piece of business which always reduced Kenny More to giggles. In the sleeve of my judge's robe I concealed a huge red-spotted handkerchief, which I used to produce at intervals and pretend to blow my nose. It was a perfect excuse to blow a raspberry, and I grasped the opportunity with both lips.

When the programme was repeated on 2 January, 1950, we had to perform it live all over again, because in those days it was not possible to make a recording for later use. A lot has been said about the transmission of live television shows, with opposing views about their virtue. Those in favour say that the adrenalin of performing live gives an artist that extra edge, but I must admit that I prefer the controlled atmosphere of a recorded show, without the air of desperate gaiety which comes with the knowledge that if you make a mistake, millions of people are going to see it.

*

I had now become a resident comedian on 'Welsh Rarebit', and from 26 January 1950 I appeared every week. There was no pantomime engagement for me during the Christmas period of 1949/50, which was no real surprise after my disastrous debut in *Dick Whittington*, and I was content to do the radio programmes and consolidate my career. The variety theatre bookings were coming in steadily, and my salary had increased to fifty pounds a week.

One week found me playing the Metropolitan, Edgware Road, one of the Syndicate Halls, and the only theatre in the group that I had not played during the tour of *Dick Whittington*.

It was a very good 'shop window' theatre to play, because it was easily accessible for all the London agents and bookers, and it had one feature that I don't think any other theatre possessed. The bar in the stalls had a huge plate glass window through which the customers could watch the acts while having a drink. This was where the men who did all the bookings could stand with large whiskies and decide the fate of the sweating performers on the other side of the glass.

The top of the bill the first week I played there was Jack Train, the impressionist, who was a regular on 'ITMA', the great wartime comedy show which starred Tommy Handley. For some reason, perhaps because there were a lot of young people in the audience, I did really well on the opening night. I was beginning to achieve a radio popularity and when I came on the audience applauded. That was what we all aimed at. It was a sure sign of recognition, and brought with it the realization that you no longer had to struggle to coax the first laughs from those all-important people out front – the paying public. And it meant that some of them had even come in especially to see you.

I did so well that week that the management moved my position further down the bill. It was the first time that I had vacated that spot that every young comic dreaded – second act on. We used to make desperate gags about our position when we came on to face the audience: 'I

wouldn't give this spot to a dry cleaner,' was a favourite
line.

One night that week I learned that Lew Grade of the Grade
Agency had been in to see me, and had liked my act. He had
left a telephone number for me to ring the following day.

When I told Norman Vaughan back at Linden Gardens,
where I still shared the flat whenever I was in London, he
said, 'Great, mate. He's a really big agent - he can get you the
Palladium.'

I got very excited and rang the Grade Agency's number first
thing the following morning and made an appointment to see
Lew and his brother Leslie the same afternoon.

I was ushered into their posh premises in Regent Street,
introduced to Leslie (who was later to become a dear friend)
and offered a seat in Lew's office. He was on the phone.

'Well, I've got the boy in the office with me now, Val,' he
said, waving his cigar at me in greeting.

Val? That has to be Val Parnell, I thought, the head of Moss
Empires and the man who puts on the Palladium shows. I began to twitch with excitement and apprehension as Lew made
a few complimentary remarks about me to Val before going
on to discuss other business. When he had put the phone
down, Lew shook my hand across the desk and asked me who
was representing me. As it happened I was between agents. I
had not been satisfied with the way things were going and had
left the Will Hammer office, a fairly small-time agency.

I told Lew that I had no agent at the moment and he sat
back in his chair and recited all the benefits which would
accrue to me if I'd sign up with his outfit. I would be put on
a sliding-scale salary, increasing on a yearly basis, and in a few
weeks' time, God willing, I could be playing the Palladium.

It was a great temptation and I almost signed there and
then as Lew wanted me to. But something held me back.
Jimmy Grafton and I had been talking the previous week
about how my career should go and we had decided that
the 'parabola' was the best way – a gentle rise and a slow
fall, rather than the 'rocket' – going straight up and, energy

spent, falling quickly. Besides, I did not think that I was ready for the Palladium, which, though it was the Mecca for every aspiring performer, was also the focus for the national press, and failure there could be fatal.

I asked Lew if I could think about the deal, and promised to come back with my answer in a couple of days. He was surprised that I had not snapped up his offer, but was gracious enough to agree to see me again.

Sleep did not come easily that night. I was doing quite nicely as I was, slowly acquiring a name on radio and gradually learning my craft on the stage. But, on the other hand, if I made a big impact at the Palladium I could almost be a star overnight. . .

The following morning I went down to see Jimmy Grafton, whose opinion I valued, and he took me out on to the golf course with him for my first-ever game. On the way around, in between retrieving balls from various inaccessible parts of the rough, we decided that in the long run and all things considered it would be better for my future career if I turned down Lew's offer.

'You'd be far better off with a smaller agent who only has a few acts. Then he could concentrate on shaping your future, nurture you, and then when you're ready – and not before - you can play the Palladium,' said Jim, sinking a long putt on the seventeenth hole.

I agreed, and went back to see Lew Grade.

When Lew heard my decision he was rather upset and shook his cigar at me. 'All right, lad,' he said. 'But one day you'll come crawling back to me.'

'I don't think so, Mr Grade,' I replied, and left his office.

Six years later, when I was starring at the London Palladium in *Rocking The Town* Lew came into my dressing-room. 'I didn't come crawling back did I, Lew?' I said. And he laughed and offered me a cigar.

*

The fact that I was now singing every week on 'Welsh Rarebit' made me a target for the song pluggers. These were the men who worked for the music publishers and it was their job to persuade artists to sing the songs published by their companies. I would frequently be visited in my dressing-room by anxious middle-aged men who would stand about a foot away from me and sing into my face their latest melody. 'My grey-haired mother' they would croon unaccompanied, or else a song about 'an old lamplighter' or 'an old cobbler' or whatever profession was considered to be romantic at the time. They were earnest gentlemen who, on closer acquaintance, proved to have a great sense of humour.

If a singer agreed to perform one of their tunes on a broadcast, they would provide a free orchestration which saved the artist paying a quite hefty sum of money, and they invariably put the singer's photograph on the front of the piano copy with the words 'as featured by so-and-so on such-and-such radio show'. There were also rumours of plug money being paid as an extra blandishment, but I was not big enough to be offered that.

I became very friendly with one of the song pluggers – a man called Leslie Simpson, who would also spare the time to run over songs he thought might be suitable for my voice, even if his company did not publish them. He taught me how to interpret a ballad rather than just belt it out, which I sometimes did out of sheer embarrassment. I was slowly becoming aware that my voice could be used to more advantage, but it was still slightly unfocused, and under pressure I was in danger of singing sharp.

However, I was now using a couple of straight songs in my stage act. 'Falling In Love With Love' was one, and 'We'll Keep A Welcome' (the theme song of 'Welsh Rarebit') was the other. My band parts soon became rather tattered as my work in the variety theatres increased. They were also getting pretty illegible because of the pencilled notes all over them. Members of the brass section in one pit orchestra would leave little notes for their counterparts in the next town on my touring schedule. 'Good for a pint, here' perhaps, when there was a long pause in the music, or 'How's Lily?' from one double bass player to another. It got so that I could hardly make out the musical notes from the pencilled notes.

The problem was solved when I was booked to appear at the Finsbury Park Empire, which in terms of our profession was the next best thing to playing the Palladium. All the big American acts were to be seen there and it was a much sought-after date.

When I put my tatty music down on the stage prior to the band call it looked very much out of place among the red and blue leather books which held the orchestral parts of the other artists, and I felt very uncomfortable when my turn came to rehearse.

'What's this lot, then?' Syd Caplan, the resident musical director, handled my little pile of scribbled notes as if they harboured some dread disease.

'I'm very sorry, Mr Caplan. I've been meaning to get some new ones done.'

He sniffed and shook his head disapprovingly. A lot of people seemed to be doing that to me, I thought miserably.

'All right, leave it to me. I'll do you a new set of books by the end of the week. These are really disgusting.'

I agreed readily, little realizing that by the time I had paid for the band books there wouldn't be much left out of my week's salary. Apparently Syd Caplan always used the same ploy when an artist turned up with music in a tatty condition. The bill came as a blow, but I have to confess that those red leather books with gold embossed letters on the front that spelt my name and the name of the instrument section of the parts it contained are still in good condition today, so in the long run it was a very wise investment.

Myra was with me for the week, along with little Jennifer, who was now twelve months old. We had booked into a small bed and breakfast hotel in Russell Square which was on the Actors' Church Union list of lodgings. It was not a very happy week for Myra, because she was left alone practically all day with the baby, and, in addition, the hotel had been freshly painted.

I have never been able to stand the smell of fresh paint and my throat became affected by it. To make matters worse, on the night that a big agent came in to see my act, I had forgotten to bring a clean shirt for the second show, with the result that I had to go on stage in the shirt in which I had performed the first house. I was nervous too, and it showed. At the end of the performance, Ted Gollop, who was the assistant to Cissie Williams, the lady responsible for booking all the acts for Moss Empires, came backstage and took me to task for the state of my shirt. Miss Williams had the final say about whether an act was fit to play the circuit and had an extremely powerful influence on the variety scene as a whole. Ted Gollop was always at her side when she came to a theatre, and was forever running through the pass door to the stage to convey her likes and dislikes to the artists concerned. There was a story going the rounds that when her pet dog died she made Ted wear a black armband.

It was quite some time before I played a Moss Empires theatre again. I heard that she had declared my act to be dirty. Whether it was because of the shirt I wore that second house, or whether the lady took a dislike to the raspberries I blew, I never found out. But to call my shaving act 'dirty' was a bit thick – after all, I always boasted that it was the cleanest act in the business.

There were some astonishingly eccentric performers doing the rounds at the same time as myself. Take Henry Vadden, for instance, who had a most unusual finish to his act. He would stand in the centre of the stage and strap on a helmet upon the top of which was a large spike. He would give a signal for the drummer in the pit to begin a dramatic roll on the tymps and the lights would go down, leaving him in a white spotlight. He would then give a cry, and from the flies above the stage, a large cartwheel would fall and he would catch it on the spike. Then he'd give the wheel a twirl and the curtains would close as it spun on the helmet.

I watched him from the wings one Monday night at the first–house performance. As the cartwheel thudded down on to his helmet I heard him utter a strangled cry as his neck disappeared into his shoulders. This was the first show of the week, remember, and he had to go through the whole business another eleven times.

There was another act that always intrigued me, and indeed I used it as the basis of an episode in my novel about the variety theatre, *Twice Brightly*. It was a lion act, and though it was billed on the theatre posters as 'a forest-bred animal', it was more likely 'Epping Forest-bred', and was practically toothless.

For the breath-taking climax to his performance, the lion's trainer would announce that the beast would now eat a hunk of raw meat which he would place on his lady assistant's chest. She lay down, the dripping joint was placed on her bosom, and the lion would commence to slobber over it as the tabs came down. What the audience at first house did not see was the battle between the trainer and the lion as he removed the meat from its jaws to be re-used in the second performance of the evening.

Then there were foot jugglers, ladies and gentlemen who lay on their backs on specially designed padded wooden supports, and balanced barrels and large, painted spheres on their feet, sometimes tossing them to a similarly positioned partner on the other side of the stage. There were incredibly daring clowns who did comedy routines on slack wires high off the ground with no safety net, pretending to be drunk and seeming about to crash to the floor at any moment. But they never did. I saw a knife-thrower who, blindfolded, would throw his shining deadly weapons all around the body of his sequin-clad assistant while she was strapped by her arms and legs to a revolving wooden wheel – and not a drop of blood to be seen at the finish. I remember a one-armed dog trainer who used to put a little black and white terrier through a most complicated routine of tricks without one word of command. As Spike Milligan remarked after he'd seen this particular turn, 'He must have had a bloody big dog in the act at one time.'

Touring the halls could be a monotonous business. The daily routine after the Monday, when all the preparatory work such as band call and setting out your dressing-room was done, was always of the same pattern.

I would arrive at the theatre at about eleven o'clock, following a leisurely nine o'clock breakfast at the digs. If the act had gone well on the Monday night I would enter the stage door with a light step, eager to revisit the scene of my success, ready with a smile for the stage door-keeper as I collected my mail, and then up the stairs to my dressing-room to read the letters at leisure. Then, back down to the stage level for a chat with the stage-manager, who usually brought me down to earth with some kind of criticism of my performance – either I'd run over time or I'd made too much mess with the shaving soap and ruined the front tabs.

Chastened, I would wait for the entry of some of the other acts and discuss what was on at the local cinema or exchange the latest showbiz gossip. 'I see Bygraves is going to play the Palladium' or 'I hear Frankie Howerd died a death at Bradford' or 'Who was the comic who was taken off the bill at Bolton?' And I'd say 'It was me,' and conversation would slacken for a while.

Then it was off to the pub for a couple of pints and a meat pie and back to the digs for a kip before first house.

On the other hand, if the act had not gone well on the previous night, I would stay in bed until lunch-time, worrying, and asking myself why I had chosen the theatre as a profession. Then, after walking through the stage door on leaden feet and surreptitiously checking the trains out of town in case I was going to be paid off, I would set out to face the audience like a Christian in Roman times entering an arena full of lions. And if I was lucky, I'd get an audience that liked what I was doing and I'd walk home to the digs that night about a foot off the ground, and the glass of stout with supper would taste like champagne and the landlady was an angel and I was going to top the bill at the London Palladium.

Then along would come Thursday night, and I'd spend the day in bed again.

It was always a relief to get away from the theatre and join in the revels at Grafton's on a Sunday night. Spike, Peter, Mike and I were fast developing a team spirit and enjoyed bouncing ideas off each other. All the time Jimmy Grafton watched approvingly, sometimes curbing our excesses with a constructive suggestion, which won him the nickname KOGVOS ('King Of Goons And Voice Of Sanity').

Peter was the only one of our quartet who had a theatrical background. His grandmother on his mother's side was a descendant of Daniel Mendoza, the Portuguese Jew who was the heavyweight champion boxer of England around the beginning of the 1800s – a time when they fought with bare fists. She was left a widow with several young children, and rather than passively bemoan her fate, started a touring revue. Her real name was Welcome, but she called herself Ma Ray and became a big attraction on the halls. Her daughter Peg, who had married a Protestant from Yorkshire, Bill Sellers, followed in her mother's footsteps, specializing in 'tableaux' with her pianist husband as her accompanist.

Oddly enough, Peter was born on 8 September 1925, exactly four years to the day after me. In his youth he became fascinated by the skill of the drummer in a band which played at the Victoria Pavilion in Ilfracombe. The theatre was managed by his uncle, and Peter used to help out with the chores. The drummer caught him playing his drums one day and, instead of giving him a good telling-off, he gave him instruction, and soon Peter was playing with some of the established dance bands. When he was eighteen he joined the RAF and was eventually posted to the Ralph Reader *Gang Show*, finishing up in India. He was often in trouble with his superiors for impersonating them – a habit we had in common. Also, like me, he had performed at the Windmill, where he had earned £25 a week – five quid more than I had got – and his name finished up along with mine on the famous board outside the theatre.

To get his first BBC Radio job, Peter rang a producer called Roy Speer, and by impersonating the voices of Kenneth Horne and Richard Murdoch, he recommended himself for an audition. For his cheek he was granted one. From then on his reputation grew apace and, as I have already recounted, we met on several radio programmes. He was a perfectionist who even at that early stage in his career was showing signs of greatness. But he was never completely happy, always feeling that he could have given a better performance.

Of the four of us, he was the most nerveless. I don't think that I ever saw him show any kind of nervousness about performing before an audience. He was always completely in command of himself and was never afraid to experiment with gags on stage. I can best illustrate this by leaping forward in time a couple of years to when Peter, Spike and myself were all performing together in a show at the Coventry Hippodrome. It was November, and the cold seemed to have seeped into the souls of the audiences who, at times, appeared to be completely baffled by what was going on up on stage.

One night Peter walked on carrying a chair and addressed the audience thus: 'I've been out shopping today, and I came across a little EP record of Christmas Carols performed by the Wally Stott Orchestra. I was so enchanted by it, I decided I'd like to share it with you.'

He then gave a nod to the electrician side-stage, who had been primed in advance to have the record ready to play over the house sound system.

The music started. Peter sat down on the chair, crossed his legs and hummed along with the music.

The audience looked at one other in complete confusion as this went on, but at the end of the music gave Peter a desultory spattering of applause.

'I knew you'd like it,' he cried, leaping from his chair. 'So let's hear the other side, shall we?'

And he sat down again as the rest of the record was played. When the music finished he got up, bowed to the audience, and brushing away an imaginary tear, walked off stage with the chair.

And I had to follow that lot with 'Bless This House'.

Spike was born on 16 April 1918 in the Military Hospital in Ahmednaga, the son of an Irish sergeant-major in the British Army. His Christian names are Terence Alan but as Michael Caine might say, 'not many people know that'. His boyhood was spent in the army barracks of India, but his father became the victim of a cut in the armed forces and at the age of forty left for England with no prospects of work.

The family settled in a terraced house in Catford, and in time Spike found himself working in a tobacco factory for thirteen shillings a week. He bought a trumpet on the instalment plan and joined a dance band in Brockley. In between gigs he did a variety of jobs after he'd got the sack from the tobacco firm for pilfering fags. He worked in a laundry and at Woolwich Arsenal as an unskilled labourer.

In June 1940 he was called up into the 56th Heavy Regiment RA at Bexhill-on-Sea. I can testify to the fact that he was a good soldier and, surprisingly enough, a very smart one, but he could never accept unnecessary regimentation and was constantly at war with the establishment. Come to think of it, he still is.

At Monte Cassino Spike was caught up in the blast of a mortar shell and was wounded and severely shell-shocked. This put an effective end to his involvement in any more fighting, and as I've already mentioned, he spent quite a long time at a psychiatric hospital near Sorrento.

After his spell with the Bill Hall Trio he got fed up with touring, and Jimmy Grafton offered him work as a script-writer. He began writing for Derek Roy – a job he hated –

and for an up-and-coming comedian, Alfred Marks. In time he was to live in a room above Grafton's which could only be reached by a ladder, so we all christened him 'The Prisoner Of Zenda'.

If I was asked to sum up Spike at this point in his career, I'd say he was a half-educated genius with an over-developed sense of the ridiculous and a healthy disrespect for the status quo. Looking back on those days, I find it hard to believe some of the wild things we got up to.

Once, when Spike and I were staying at the Mapleton Hotel in Piccadilly, he bet me that I would not run around the block in my vest and underpants. He underestimated me, I'm afraid, and fortified by several brandies, I set off. It was early evening as I ran out of the room, down the stairs and out through the main door into the street. Fortunately it was pouring with rain, and I made my way around the block with only a few ladies of easy virtue to cheer my efforts and offer me various rewards for my athletic prowess, at reasonable prices. Nobody else took a blind bit of notice, and I padded back into the hotel past the commissionaire who nodded at me in a friendly way. 'Been for a run, Harry?' he said.

When I got back upstairs, very wet and extremely short of breath, Spike had locked the door. It took twenty minutes of pleading before he opened it again.

There was a time when everyone seemed to be wearing duffel coats. Spike had one and so did I, and they were rarely off our backs. I developed a way of buttoning mine right up over my head, so that I looked like Norman Vaughan's 'lion-tamer's father' in the gag I did in his act at Bolton. It became a party trick which I'd do at the drop of a hat, until one afternoon it came unstuck.

Spike, Johnny Mulgrew, Peter and myself were having a meal in a rather posh café in Golders Green, and after we'd eaten, the other lads said, 'Go on, Harry, do your duffel coat bit.'

In a trice I buttoned my coat over my head in my now familiar way and proceeded to make Goonish noises from within. I kept this up for several minutes. Then, gradually, I became aware that the place seemed to have gone very quiet. I opened one of the toggles and peeped out. The others had gone, the bill was on a saucer before me, unpaid, and the café owner was standing at the table, glaring at me. I struggled out of my coat, red-faced with embarrassment. Not a word was said as I fumbled through my pockets looking for money to pay the bill. I had just enough, without a tip, and the whole transaction took place in an eerie silence as the rest of the customers looked on. As I reached the door I turned and blew a raspberry, but it was a Pyrrhic victory at best.

Another time, after a liquid lunch at Bertorelli's Restaurant in Shepherd's Bush, Spike noticed that there was an undertaker's parlour a couple of doors away. He promptly lay down outside on the pavement in the duffel coat, with his eyes closed and his arms crossed over his chest, as the rest of us hammered on the door calling 'Shop!'

Mike Bentine was the only one of us with a 'pedigree'. He was born to a Peruvian physicist father and an English mother, and we always claimed that he was the only Peruvian born on the Watford by-pass. He had been educated at Eton and the Lycée in Paris, spoke several languages fluently, and claimed a degree in nuclear physics. During the war he had trained as a pilot, but a vaccination which went wrong affected his eyesight and instead he became an Intelligence Officer with a Polish Squadron.

He seemed to be capable of anything – he was an accomplished swordsman, a fine shot with a pistol, an expert with the long bow, a very good artist and an excellent cook. We could never fault his prowess in these areas, although we frequently tried, and if sometimes we became suspicious of this wealth of talent we had to accept the fact that he was indeed an extremely versatile young man.

His contribution to our evenings of comedy experimentation at Jimmy's pub was immense, and his enthusiasm was boundless. Yet there was the beginning of a rift developing between Spike and himself about who had thought up some particular piece of funny business, or how a theme should be developed. It wasn't a yawning chasm, because they both respected each other, but there were differences between them. There was a whiff of the establishment about Bentine which I found fascinating, but Spike was, perhaps, less attracted by it.

Something else to bear in mind was the fact that Mike was the first of the four of us to make an impression in the West End. He scored a big success in *Starlight Roof* at the Hippodrome, with an act in which he used the back of a chair as a prop. It was a brilliant performance in which he used this most unlikely piece of carpentry as a comb, a flag, a plough and God knows what else. Peter and I were now making some headway in the halls, but Spike had not yet worked out a solo act for himself.

Mike was always good company, so when one Sunday, early on in our acquaintance, he invited me to spend the day with him at the house of a recently acquired girl-friend, I accepted readily.

She lived with her family in the outer suburbs of London, and as neither of us had a car, we took the train. It was a lovely summer afternoon, and the house was quite grand. The company consisted of the girl's mother and father and an aunt, who were all dazzled by the brilliance of Mike's conversation.

Throughout a beautifully cooked meal he regaled us with stories of his days in repertory with Robert Atkins, and when it came to playing a spot of croquet on the lawn he beat everybody, performing wonders with his mallet. At tea, which was sumptuous and extremely filling – especially after our huge lunch – he enthralled us with tales of his adventures in the Air Force. By the end of our visit everyone, including myself, was captivated by Mike's wit and eloquence.

Farewells were said, and then the three ladies decided to walk us to the station, leaving the father behind. Mike enlivened the short walk with descriptions of ballets he had seen, and as we walked on to the gravel leading to the station platform, he decided to show us Nijinsky's famous leap as performed in *The Spectre Of The Rose*.

He took a little run and leapt into the air. Unfortunately, the amount of food Mike had consumed throughout the day – the roast beef and apple tart at lunch and the pastries and the boiled ham at tea – proved too much, and as he took off he gave vent to a blast from his nether regions. It was gargantuan, and had it been properly harnessed it would have propelled him over the roof of the railway station. It seemed to me that the shock of it actually delayed his return to earth, exactly like Nijinsky's celebrated leap.

I immediately collapsed in hysterics against the wall of the station, and the three ladies, who were standing watching arm in arm, abruptly turned around and began to walk off without a backward glance. Mike followed them for a few steps, making little raspberry sounds with his mouth in a vain attempt to convince them that he had made the sound from that end. But their retreating backs offered no forgiveness. He turned to where I lay, kicking my heels in the gravel in helpless, uncontrollable laughter, and, seeing the funny side of the incident himself, he joined in the hysteria.

Another ex-serviceman who used to join in the cut-and-thrust of the impromptu comedy sessions was Larry Stephens, who eventually collaborated on 'The Goon Show' scripts with Spike. He had been an officer with Brigadier Orde Wingate in Burma and had seen a lot of action.

This was the cast which was slowly but inexorably heading towards the creation of a comedy show which we hoped the BBC might accept as a series. However, before this happened I had to do more slogging around the provinces and the London surburban theatres.

It was not exactly an uneventful time for me; I was fired on by an air pistol wielded by some lunatic in the gallery at the Grand Theatre, Clapham; a penny struck me forcibly on the forehead when I was playing the Hippodrome, Wigan; and once I had to do my act wearing a dinner jacket and brown tweed trousers. I had forgotten that it was half-day closing and when I went to collect my soap-stained dress pants from the cleaners that afternoon, I had found the place shut. 'I'm trying to set a new trend,' I said lamely to the audience, but I don't think they were ready to accept the joke.

Myra had decided that touring every week with the baby was not really good for either of them, and so until I got an engagement that enabled me to stay in the same place for a reasonable length of time, she opted to stay at home with her parents in West Cross, Swansea, and I would join her there at weekends.

As the year 1950 rolled into autumn, a request came for me to do pantomime in Hull. It was far enough away from my less-than-successful appearance in *Dick Whittington* and I was offered the part of Simple Simon – a much easier role to play than Dame. The subject was *Jack and The Beanstalk* and the venue was the New Theatre, which showed straight plays for the rest of the year. I accepted the offer with alacrity and Myra was delighted at the prospect of the three of us being together for a good spell.

The digs we had booked into must have slipped through the net of the Actors' Church Union because they were not very good. When we lit a fire in our room the smoke always blew back down the chimney and nearly suffocated us. We decided to move to a very nice little hotel called the White House, which we could not really afford, but we were worried about Jennifer's health. It was a great idea as it turned out, and we were very well looked after. Myra's parents came up from Swansea to spend Christmas with us, and they were able to give Myra a break from looking after the baby.

The pantomime was much easier than *Dick Whittington* and I had no trouble learning the part of Simple Simon. The Dame was played properly and traditionally by Alan Modley, the brother of the more famous Yorkshire comedian, Albert Modley. Gordon Norville, who was a rather camp Demon

King, also produced the pantomime. The Principal Boy was Valerie Ashton, who was later to marry Sid James, and the Princess was a lady called Primrose Gordon. The Giant was a large gentleman who made 'Fee-fi-fo-fum' seem like an invitation. It was a nice, happy show and I can only remember one instance when something went wrong with the production.

In the prologue to the show, Gordon – dressed all in green, with sequins stuck to his eyelids – had to make a speech, lit by a green spotlight, about what he was going to do to Simple Simon and his mother when he caught them. At the conclusion of the diatribe he disappeared through a trapdoor in the stage and then up went the lights and on came the full company to sing the opening chorus.

One night something went wrong with the trapdoor and Gordon only disappeared up to his shoulders. The lights went up and revealed him swearing away at the stage-manager while the boys and girls of the chorus danced around him. Suddenly the trap moved again, and he struck his chin on the stage as he finally dropped out of sight. His cursing could be heard throughout the theatre.

While we were in Hull, Len Lightowler, who had been in the 'Sicily Billies' concert party, came with his wife, Maude, to see the show, and Myra and I went over to Leeds to stay with them on a couple of weekends.

I went back to the hotel one night to find Jennifer drunk. She had somehow got into a room where a private cocktail party was being held and had gone around drinking out of the sherry glasses on the tables. I must say that she slept well that night, and for the first time in weeks, so did we.

CHAPTER TEN

Those Crazy People

On 3 February 1951 I travelled down to London on the night train to make a trial recording of 'The Junior Crazy Gang', produced at the BBC by Pat Dixon. At last the perseverance of Spike, Jimmy and the rest of us had paid off and we had a chance to make a break-through in comedy. For three years the recordings we had made at Grafton's had been turned down by the BBC as being 'too way-out'; but now the powers that be had relented.

We were not too happy about the full title, which was 'The Junior Crazy Gang – starring those crazy people, the Goons'. The Crazy Gang, as everyone at the time knew, was a collection of very funny veteran acts – Flanagan and Allen, Nervo and Knox, Naughton and Gold, and on occasions, Monsewer Eddie Grey. They were noted for their shows at the Victoria Palace and for them, nothing was sacred. We admired them but we didn't think that we should be called the 'Junior' anything – we felt we had our own identity, and didn't want to share anyone else's.

I cannot now remember what that first show was all about, except that it was fast and furious and disjointed, containing musical items by the Stargazers, Ray Ellington and Max Geldray. After the show we weren't sure whether we would get a series or not.

Meanwhile, on the theatrical side of my career, I was

taken up by George and Alfred Black, the sons of the great
impresario George Black, who had controlled the gigantic
Moss General Theatre Corporation during the 1930s and
the war period. They had their father's flair for putting on
shows, and as ex-servicemen themselves, they had a soft spot
for entertainers from the forces. They signed me up for some
variety dates and their big season at the Opera House, Blackpool. This was the Palladium of the summer season theatres,
and the shows they mounted there were equal to any big
West End production. I was thrilled because it meant that
Myra and Jennifer could have a good long holiday by the
seaside with all expenses paid, so to speak. The show was
to be called *Happy Go Lucky* and would run from early
summer until the Blackpool lights were switched on. The
stars of the show were Vera Lynn, George and Bert Bernard,
the American mime artists, and Jack Radcliffe, a Scottish comedian who specialized in 'old men' parts. There was also
the spectacular Jimmy Currie's Waterfalls – a scene which
involved thousands of gallons of water. How the stage was
not flooded every night I'll never know.

In between variety dates and the opening of the summer
show, I did quite a lot of broadcasts, including 'Variety
Bandbox', 'Welsh Rarebit' and 'Music Hall'. Then came the
news that Spike, Peter, Mike and I had been waiting for. The
BBC had granted us six shows, the first one to be recorded on
Sunday, 27 May, to be transmitted the following day at 6.45
pm on the Home Service.

On the strength of this news I decided it was time to buy
another car, preferably one which had rear windows that
stayed in position when I drove it. I happened to be home
in Swansea that week and Myra and I made a tour of the
various garages offering second-hand cars for sale. She was
keen on an Austin Princess which would have knocked me
back £900, but, with uncharacteristic caution, I settled for an
Austin Ten for about £300. At last I was mobile – no more
waiting for trains on draughty stations – I could head for
home as soon as my week's work was finished. The car was

in good condition and was sturdy enough to accept the large cabin trunk which carried all my clothes.

It was in this magnificent vehicle that I set out for the first recording of the new BBC comedy series, which was to be at the Aeolian Hall, Bond Street. I was no stranger to the place, having previously broadcast many programmes from the studio. For the rest of the series I had to drive down to London from Blackpool on the Saturday night to arrive in time for the Sunday morning rehearsal, which prompted the rest of the cast to refer to me as 'he who drives through the night'.

When I arrived I was greeted by our producer, Dennis Main Wilson, who was to collect a fine crop of stomach ulcers as time went by as the result of trying to handle the four of us. Pat Dixon, having set up the pilot programme, was content to let Dennis take over the actual series. I think we began the first read-through of the script at about 10.30 am. This was an exciting moment for us and we were all in a state of near hysteria, laughing at lines in the script whether or not they were funny. It was the first time I had seen any of the show written down because I had been travelling around the country so much, but it didn't take us long to get a rhythm going. We had become used to each other's timing during the sessions at Jimmy's pub, and the first signs of the almost extrasensory perception we were later to develop began to show.

The 'warm-up' for the show consisted of a string of mad routines. I came on and began to sing 'Falling In Love With Love' accompanied by Ray Ellington's pianist, Dick Katz, and as soon as I had sung a few bars Peter came on, removed my braces and walked off the stage with them. As I continued with the song, Spike made an entrance and, for no reason, took an exaggerated bow. I then sang the final top notes, stepped forward, and pulled his trousers down.

Then there was a bit of a jam session with the Ellington Quartet and Peter on drums and Spike on trumpet. When the red light flashed, on came Andrew Timothy, the regular BBC announcer, to tell the audience that the recording was about to begin. Tim, as everybody called him, had been a chaplain in the 'Para' brigade, wore a monocle and looked absolutely fed up with the whole business.

I remember little about the show itself, but in a book by Alfred Draper called *The Story Of The Goons* (Everest Books, 1976) he recalls that we did a sketch about BRM, the racing car made in Britain, which was a target for many jokes.

Bentine, as a Grand Prix entrepreneur, says to Sellers, 'Here's five thousand pounds. I want you to go to Italy and bring back the finest motoring brains that money can buy.'

Peter races away on a sound effect, and Mike remarks, 'Three weeks later he arrived back with a glass jar. In it were the finest motoring brains that money could buy.'

In the show we also did a parody of a very popular radio serial, 'Dick Barton Special Agent', which finished like this:

PETER (as Barton): Look, they've thrown something through the door!

HARRY (as Jock): What'll we do?

PETER: Quick men – put your fingers in your ears.

Then came a very loud explosion.

Listen again tomorrow to 'Dick Barton's Special Funeral'.

The show finished with Mike declaiming the following words to the accompaniment of 'Land Of Hope And Glory':

Today the motherland can still raise her proud face to the skies and say . . .

HARRY: HEEEEELLPP!!

It was not vintage stuff, and a lot of what we did mystified more than entertained the audience in the studio. I also sang a song on the show – I've forgotten which ballad it was, but I do know that by having to dash from one microphone where I was performing a sketch with the other three to another nearer the orchestra, I became a bit breathless and consequently didn't sing too well.

Afterwards, Michael Standing, the Head of Variety, told Dennis Main Wilson that I should do no more singing on the programme because I was out of tune. When Jimmy Grafton conveyed the news to me a few days later, I began to wonder whether I should continue to sing or pack it in altogether.

I now had a new agent, Frank Barnard, a canny old Geordie from Newcastle who had at one time managed the affairs of Jack Hylton, the famous dance-band leader. He was Derek Roy's agent, and after Jimmy's talk with me before I turned down Lew Grade's offer, it seemed a good idea to put my career in his hands. He had a small agency, he was shrewd, and above all he was respected in the business for his integrity. We had no contract, we just shook hands on the deal, and I stayed with him until he died about fifteen years ago. Jimmy became his partner, and between the two of them they piloted me through the dangerous waters of the profession.

During the year I had played Dudley Hippodrome, a beautiful theatre in the Midlands owned by Bob and Maurice Kennedy. Bob became a particular friend of mine, and he too was eventually to work for me, and at the age of eighty-two, still does, thank God.

When the time came to go to Blackpool for the first rehearsals, Myra packed the car with her typical thoroughness. Before our marriage she had worked in the rag trade, and when she folds a garment, brother, it stays folded. The interior of the car was loaded right up to window level, and on the top of all the luggage, Jennifer was placed in a carry cot. It's a tribute to Myra's expertise that throughout the long trip from Swansea to Blackpool, not one piece of luggage became dislodged. However, the cabin trunk – which I had personally strapped to the open boot – fell off three times.

We had chosen our accommodation carefully, because it was going to be a long season and we wanted the three of us to be as comfortable as possible. When we arrived in Blackpool, Myra pronounced herself very satisfied with the rooms and Jennifer seemed to be more contented than she had been at other places where we had stayed.

It was always a nightmare for a mother and child to travel around the country on tour in those days. Some goods were still in short supply, bread was rationed, and so were sweets. There were no huge supermarkets where you could buy everything all under the one roof – you had to shop around for what you required. It was essential to have a place for washing and drying the nappies as there were no disposable ones then, and prams in the hallway were discouraged in some digs. Myra always seemed to manage without a fuss, and had the happy knack of making friends with even the most taciturn landladies. Except, that is, for the one in Harrow.

Before I let Myra unpack the car I took her on a tour of Blackpool, to show her the Tower and the famous Promenade. It was getting dark and the lights were on. There was a bustle and excitement about the town – an 'all the fun of the fair' atmosphere. Everywhere there were posters for the big shows and famous faces grinned down from the hoardings. Arthur Askey, Norman Evans and Vera Lynn were just a few of the big names who were appearing at the many theatres Blackpool had to offer. There was the smell of candyfloss and beer, and people strolled arm in arm along the seafront, savouring the salty evening air. It was brash and noisy and we both loved it.

'Mind you,' said Myra, on the way back to the digs, 'Swansea Sands takes a bit of beating.'

She always sticks up for her home town. When I took her abroad to Italy and she had her first glimpse of the Bay of Naples she remarked, 'Very nice, but Swansea Bay is just as pretty. Smaller perhaps, but just as pretty.'

Backstage at the Opera House the following morning I met the people with whom I was going to work for the next few months. Vera Lynn was in her dressing-room with her hair in curlers, and was warm, friendly and completely down to earth. She made me very welcome and introduced me to Harry Lewis, her husband. The next person I met was Jack Radcliffe, a smartly dressed Scot, who was to teach me a lot about repose on stage. If I moved at the wrong time in a sketch with him, he would actually hit me. It's a great way to learn.

George and Bert Bernard had been a big hit at the London Palladium. Their act consisted of miming to records by Bing Crosby and the Andrews Sisters, among others, and they were also very good dancers. Bert was married to Zoë Gail, an English revue artist, and was great fun. It was the first time I had encountered any American show business performers and I was fascinated by their stories about Hollywood and the sexual proclivities of some of the stars. From their tales, it was obvious that sex was in its infancy in Britain.

They were both friendly and outgoing, but George, I discovered later, could get a bit temperamental and Bert had to calm him down. However, on this, our first meeting, they gave me a warm welcome.

On the enormous stage the hands were busy setting up the scenery for the run of the show, getting all the sets into position in the flies with cries of 'Up on your short bit, Charlie' or 'Down on your long – all right, tie off', as the stage-manager and the producer supervised their efforts. This side of the theatre has always mystified me, probably because I never wear my glasses on stage and consequently can't see what's going on. But the very smell of backstage never fails to thrill me. It's a combination of dust, sweat, glue, size, paint and rosin, the hint of perfume from a passing chorus girl, and for me, a tinge of fear – especially in a theatre that's new to me.

Alec Shanks, the producer, greeted me and introduced me to the stage-manager, Dan, a tall man with a military moustache who, like all the best of his kind, was unflappable and extremely competent. When I had met everybody it was obvious that I was going to have a good time, and that's how it worked out.

I was actually given a song and dance number to do, and my Uncle George's tap dancing lessons came in handy for a soft-shoe shuffle, with the ladies of the chorus backing me up. The song was 'Toot-toot-tootsie' in a Jolson medley, and a photograph taken of me at the time shows a still reasonably slim Secombe in the costume of a yellow bowler hat and a check suit.

Working with Jack Radcliffe in sketches could be painful, as I've mentioned, but he was a great character actor as well as a comedian and he had a good singing voice. His permanent 'feed' was Helen Norman, an accomplished actress who was never thrown by Jack's frequent departures from the script. What I learned more than anything from both of them was not to indulge in private jokes on stage.

'There's nothing more annoying to an audience, son, than to see somebody laughing on stage and not being allowed in on the joke,' he said to me once.

I could hardly hear what he said for the ringing in my ears. He had given me a hefty clout on the side of my head for giggling in the sketch we had just performed. Of course he was right, but it was a bruising way to learn.

He also helped me to develop a better dress sense. I had always bought clothes off the peg, and although Myra always saw that I was neat and tidy, my wardrobe was not extensive or varied – a sports coat I had bought in Bath in the *Magpie* days and a suit from the thirty shilling tailors in Swansea was about it. Jack had a tailor friend in Glasgow who came down and measured me for my very first hand-made suit. It was a great success, and when I wore it to the 'Goon Show' recording I was greeted with cries of 'Secombe's a pouf' from my colleagues. What I really needed, though, was something to protect my ears from Jack's heavy-handed assaults on stage.

Someone else who taught me a lot was Norman Evans – the famous 'over the garden wall' comedian who was the star of the show in our sister theatre, the Winter Gardens. He was an extremely generous man and looked after the members of his company as if they were his own family. He would sometimes hire a coach and take everybody in the cast, including the stage-hands and the orchestra, on a trip into the lovely countryside which surrounds Blackpool. A sit-down meal would be arranged at an hotel, and everyone was his guest. Then he'd pick somebody at random and ask them to make a speech, because he believed that everybody should be able to express themselves in public.

I was lucky enough to be invited along on several of these occasions, and Myra and Jennifer came too. For me Norman offered a glimpse of how a star should behave – with respect for those who worked with him, and maintaining a visible presence in the theatre, not shut away in his dressing-room in splendid isolation, but accessible to all. It worked for Norman because he always had a trouble-free company and no one ever took advantage of his good nature.

I found out later on in my career that the danger of a long-running show is that 'cliques' may begin to form within the cast – and bad feeling can sour the whole season. Most of the trouble arises from insecurity. Someone might feel that he or she is being upstaged in a certain scene, or a song sung by a supporting member of the cast is being ruined by a scene change in the middle of it. If their complaints are ignored they become resentful, and the company may then divide itself up into factions for and against. On the other hand, if they feel they can approach the person who is leading the cast and express their feelings openly, something can be done to smooth out the differences before they start to affect the show. Because there's no doubt that an unhappy company communicates its unhappiness to the audience. The people out front may not know what the reason is, but inevitably they begin to feel uneasy. End of lecture!

Whenever we could Myra and I used to drive into the Trough of Bowland, a beautiful part of the country which is not too far from Blackpool. Jennifer loved these outings where we took a picnic basket and got away from the noise of the resort. My parents came up for a couple of weeks with us and so did Myra's Mum and Dad. The Austin Ten used to get a bit crowded with all of us crammed inside, so I used that as an excuse to buy a larger car.

I had become friendly with a car dealer near the theatre, and one day he showed me a second-hand vehicle which had just come on the market. It was a big black American Packard with a canvas top which folded back, turning it into an open tourer – the sort of car which I used to drool over in the Hollywood movies. It had a 'straight eight' engine with a satisfying rumble, and you could have held a dance in the back. Myra had reservations about the colour, but the salesman said he would be delighted to have it resprayed any colour we liked. We chose light grey, and when I took delivery of it a week later I was like a little schoolboy. My dreams were slowly coming true.

All through the summer I had to drive down to London for the 'Goon Show' recordings which were now billed as 'Crazy People'. The option of another six more shows was taken up on 18 June 1951 and later an option for five more was signed.

I used to leave Blackpool at the crack of dawn on the Sunday morning, and I revelled in the pleasure of driving a powerful car on almost deserted roads. My first port of call when I got to London was Grafton's, where Jimmy and Dorothy would provide coffee and bacon and eggs. I would then have a kip on their sofa in their private sitting-room upstairs until the time came for me to leave for the first read-through of the script at the BBC studio.

This was always the best part of the day for me, because I had no idea of what I had to do in the show until I got to the studio. My contribution to the writing of the script was fairly negligible, especially now that I was up in Blackpool, and I was just happy to be in the show. When we met up, we spent the first half-an-hour swapping gags and generally behaving like kids in school at playtime. Then Dennis Main Wilson would try to get some semblance of discipline into the proceedings, which was not easy. Bentine might be standing on his head demonstrating some new yoga position, Peter would perhaps be practising on Ray Ellington's bongo drums, and Spike would either be playing his trumpet or bashing out jazz chords on the piano. As for me, I'd be blowing raspberries or belting out a couple of strangled top 'C's.

Once the read-through of the script was over we'd go off to the nearest pub for a few lunch-time drinks and a snack, and then we'd return to the studio for a run-through with music and effects at four o'clock. Then there was time for a look at the Sunday papers in the stalls, or a nap, or both.

The script took on a new dimension with the addition of the musical links and the sound effects. There was always a 'spot-effects' man behind a screen with a miniature door with a knocker on it, half coconut shells for horses' hooves, a swannee whistle, a rattle as used by football fans, and anything else that Spike or Mike had decreed. In the sound booth an array of turntables were set up with all kinds of records of weird and wonderful noises, all ready to go. This was in the days before tape came into use and the sound engineers had to work with discs – 78s which had been marked up ready for the needle to fall into the exact groove required. Spike would perhaps want the sound of Big Ben mixed with a chicken cackling, so the engineer would need two turntables going at the same time. Sometimes four or five machines would all be going together with the poor fellow going berserk to keep up with all the effects – like a juggler spinning plates on the top of bamboo poles and running from one to the other to keep the momentum going so that none of them fell off.

The 'warm-up' was sometimes funnier than the show, because the gags were mostly visual and the studio audience did not have to strain to hear what was being said. That was the main criticism of those early 'Crazy People' shows – the dialogue was delivered at a tremendous rate and in so many different accents that it was frequently hard to understand. It was a common saying among the members of the cast that we had to listen to the repeats ourselves to find out what the show was all about.

After the performance there would be a post-mortem, and that was when the difference of opinion between Spike and Mike would sometimes surface. There were never big rows, it was usually the interpretation of a character, or coming in too soon, or someone else's lines that was the cause of contention.

As soon as the show was over we'd go back to Grafton's or perhaps Peter would ask us up to his place in Finchley. I never stayed too late because I had to drive back to Blackpool. Myra had someone with her every weekend to help with Jennifer, but I always felt guilty about leaving her. Still, it was important to get the exposure on radio even if the money was not very much.

Every Sunday my dressing-room at the Opera House was used by the star of the concert which went on every week during the season. I would always leave an array of drinks out on the dressing-table with a note telling the temporary occupant to help himself, with the result that I had quite a collection of thank-you notes from celebrities. This was a practice I kept up whenever I played a theatre in which my room was used in a similar way. In 1953, at the same Opera House, I had one note which I still cherish: 'Thanks for the drink, Harry. Love, Frank.' Sinatra had drunk out of one of my glasses! The funniest note was from Russ Conway, who wrote, 'I don't drink, but thanks for the offer. I let the tap run for half-an-hour.'

A well-furnished dressing-room can make a week in variety go much more quickly, and for a run of several months it is essential that your comfort is assured. In the Opera House, I had a very nice room with a chintz-covered armchair and settee and matching patterned curtains at the windows. Vera had made her room very comfortable indeed, and I often nipped in to have a cup of tea with her and Harry. She was a lovely lady to work with and is still the same today. The audiences worshipped her, and she held them in the palm of her hand as soon as she walked out on stage. She closed the show – nobody could possibly follow her.

I used to watch George and Bert Bernard's act as often as I could from the wings – with the permission of Dan, the stage-manager, of course. They relied on an off-stage assistant to put the records on at the right time, in the right order and at the right speed, and to his credit he never missed a cue. Mind you, I think George would have throttled him if he had.

George himself used to give the management a few heart attacks. Every weekend he flew to Paris where he had a flat, and sometimes the plane would be delayed. The whole cast would hold its collective breath until we heard the news that he had arrived at the stage door. He must have had a special clause written into his contract to allow him to do it, but it gave poor old Bert some stomach-churning moments.

The shaving act was still the main part of my performance and I was beginning to get fed up with it, but nothing could beat it for that second spot, and so it stayed. My singing was slowly improving, and the large orchestra was a joy to work with. My previous doubts about my voice had evaporated and I had regained some of my confidence after what Michael Standing had said.

In September, a few weeks before the show finished, I heard that I had been picked for the Royal Command Performance. This was something that I had dreamed about but never expected would happen to me. Vera Lynn and Jack Radcliffe and his partner, Helen, were also to be in the show, and so was Norman Evans from the Winter Gardens. The performance was to be on 29 November 1951 at London's Victoria Palace Theatre in the presence of King George VI and Queen Elizabeth. I could think of nothing else for weeks, and when the time came for the end of the summer season, my regret at leaving Blackpool was lightened by the excitement of the impending Royal Command.

The only time I had ever seen the King was when he drove quickly through Carthage after the end of the North African campaign, and then I didn't recognize him. On 29 November I'd be able to take a good look at him, and he would be watching me. This was the frightening part. Every old pro I spoke to said the same thing: 'The audience always look up to the Royal Box to see if They are laughing, and if so, they'll laugh too. If They're not, they won't.'

I drove the Packard home to Swansea, eager to show it off, and the journey at first was infinitely more comfortable than it had been in the Austin Ten. Then it began to rain, and we discovered we had a leak in the canvas roof. We arrived at Myra's parents' house somewhat damp, but happy to be home.

I stood side-stage at the Victoria Palace on the afternoon of Monday, 29 November, my mouth agape at the line-up of stars. It was dress-rehearsal time, and the stage and stalls were packed with celebrities. Gracie Fields was there – I had once worked the spotlight for her act in Rome when I was with the Central Pool of Artists. Then there was Florence Desmond; Frances Day; Adelaide Hall from the CSE show in Germany; Charlie Kunz, the man every NAAFI pianist aspired to imitate; Johnny Hutch and the Seven Volants – his brother was the clown who had broken his ankle on the first night of *Over the Page* at the Argentina Theatre in Rome. The Crazy Gang – after whom the four 'Goons' had been so reluctantly named – were easing the tension of the moment with some earthy jokes. Gordon Richards, the famous jockey, was in the stalls along with Joe Davis, the snooker player. Kenneth Horne and Richard Murdoch from the radio show 'Much Binding In The Marsh' were chatting together; Cicely Courtneidge was there, too. 'Professor' Jimmy Edwards, my mate from the Windmill, waved his trombone in greeting.

Arthur English nodded in my direction. Vera Lynn smiled at me, and a heavy hand clipped my earhole. 'Hello, son,' said Jack Radcliffe.

The Royal Box was bedecked with flowers, but we had received the sad news that the King was too ill to attend the performance. However, Her Majesty Queen Elizabeth would be coming, and the show was to go ahead. It was a tremendous bill, and included celebrities from the world of sport as well as show business. Apart from the ones already mentioned, also taking part were Stanley Matthews, every soccer fan's hero; MacDonald Bailey, the West Indian runner; Sydney Wooderson, the famous athlete; and the Cambridge Boat Crew.

I had already done my rehearsal in the morning, and as usual I was the second spot comic. The evening arrived – my first Royal Command Performance. The opening scene was from the Blackpool Opera House show and I was glad of the familiarity of the props as I waited for the fanfare which announced the entrance of the royal party. I stood to attention as a soldier should when the national anthem was played, and then went into a frenzy of lathering in preparation for my act.

Standing in the wings with my little table with the shaving gear on, I was reminded forcibly of my Windmill audition, and of that day years ago when I made the lads laugh in the tent at Eboli. Then I remembered that Frankie Howerd had suffered badly in this same spot on the bill the previous year. My knees began to shake as I heard the opening bars of 'I'm Just Wild About Harry'. I said to myself, 'Myra's out front' – and I grabbed my table and walked into the spotlight.

'Hello, folks,' I said.